Monty Don &
Derry Moore
Spanish Gardens

Monty Don & Derry Moore
Spanish Gardens

BBC
BOOKS

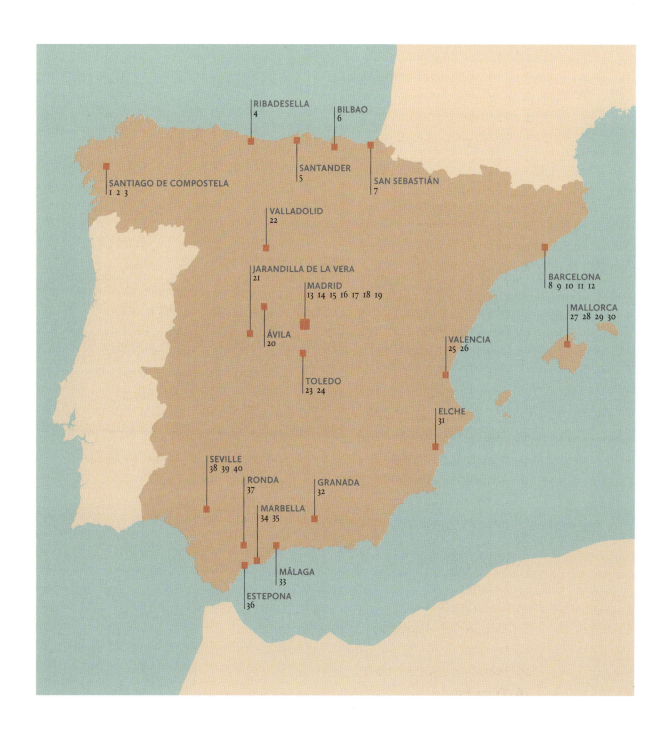

RIBADESELLA
4

BILBAO
6

SANTANDER
5

SAN SEBASTIÁN
7

SANTIAGO DE COMPOSTELA
1 2 3

VALLADOLID
22

JARANDILLA DE LA VERA
21

MADRID
13 14 15 16 17 18 19

BARCELONA
8 9 10 11 12

MALLORCA
27 28 29 30

ÁVILA
20

VALENCIA
25 26

TOLEDO
23 24

ELCHE
31

SEVILLE
38 39 40

RONDA
37

GRANADA
32

MARBELLA
34 35

MÁLAGA
33

ESTEPONA
36

Contents

Introduction *9*

Introduction

FOR MANY YEARS, I HAVE TRAVELLED – USUALLY WITH MY COLLABORATOR AND FRIEND Derry Moore – visiting, filming and writing about gardens all over the world. Of course, this needs no more justification than the sheer pleasure of seeing beautiful gardens, but I have always viewed these journeys as doing more than that. By visiting a nation's gardens, you have a distinctive key to unlock an understanding, or least a unique insight, of its culture.

I confess that my knowledge of Spanish gardens was severely limited. I was a long-time admirer of the work of the great garden designer Fernando Caruncho, and had visited the Alhambra, the Real Alcázar in Seville and a few private gardens made by British people living in Spain, but that was pretty much it.

The truth is that most people visit Spain to go on holiday, especially to the Mediterranean south, with its reliably baking sun that is so enticingly at odds with the northern climate and its attendant horticultural lushness. For the average Brit taking a hard-earned holiday on the Costa del Sunshine, gardens and gardening could not be further from their minds.

But Spain is full of fascinating and beautiful gardens. It is a huge country, over twice the size of the UK, yet with around two thirds of the British population. This is made more dramatic by the relative emptiness of much of the interior. Of course, 'empty' is a loaded word, because not only do people live there but it is also rich in wildlife of all kinds, as well as some of the most beautiful scenery in Europe.

Spain's story of human occupation and development is as old as any in Europe, but its history is powerfully marked by the period of Al-Andalus, or the Arab occupation and rule that ran from 711 to the final exit from the Alhambra at the beginning of 1492. Inevitably, almost 800 years of a dominant

culture leaves a deep and lasting influence on its gardens. The concept of the paradise garden, an enclosed and richly sensuous haven against the harshness of climate and geography, expresses itself most lastingly in the patios of Andalucía, where the garden becomes the centre of family and social life, and yet also private and protected. Twenty-first-century Spanish designers have integrated the patio with Moorish orchards and use water to create truly modern gardens that honour this deeply engrained thousand-year-old heritage.

By the beginning of the seventeenth century, Spain ruled half the known world. The Habsburg Empire spread from northern Europe through central Europe, down through Italy to Sicily, and Spain controlled much of what we know as North and South America, as well as the Philippines. Plants from the New World and from the Far East came to Spain first, mainly via Seville, before spreading across the rest of Europe. This changed the way that gardens looked for ever.

The formal parterres of the vast monastic royal palace of El Escorial are a green leavening to the austerity of the granite building.

We tend to talk and perhaps think of Spain as one united country, but throughout its history, Spain has been more divided than joined as a nation. It is significant that its first strong national ruler, Charles V, could not speak Spanish when he came to the throne and his son Philip II, who ruled at the time when immeasurable wealth poured in from the newly colonised Americas, was for a while married to Mary Tudor and thus king of England. The capital, Madrid, was created as such by Philip as late as the 1570s. Until then, Spain was a loose amalgam of principalities, and in many ways their union remains faltering if not fragile.

In modern history, Catalans, Basques and Galicians still feel strong cultural identities with distinct languages, their first loyalties to their region rather than to Spain. I asked our driver in Barcelona, younger than my children, if she would vote for an independent Catalonia. She replied that she might not because Catalonia was short of water and if separate, 'We might be beholden to Spain for water.' The 'we' was very telling. That pride in regional identity inevitably shapes and influences gardens.

The Second World War has to some extent cast a veil over the horrors of the Spanish Civil War that tore the country apart in the 1930s and which still leaves a profound mark today. Spain was desperately poor and the majority of the population could not afford the luxury of growing anything other than food. However, the garden designer and historian Mónica Luengo told me that after Franco's death in 1975, there was an explosion of creativity in garden design, as in all creative fields, though the results went largely unvisited and unacknowledged by the millions of tourists flocking into the country.

Gardens always relate to geographical position and identity. They have plants that are essentially local. In Spain, the geographic and climatic diversity and range is huge. So the Mediterranean gardens are dominated by plants that can cope with hot, dry summers (as long as they have mild, wet winters) but which are completely unsuitable in the interior of the country with its violent extremes of climate and weather. The green lushness of the northwest is more akin to Cornwall or the Gulf Stream coast of western Scotland than it is to Andalucía.

The book is divided into three sections, covering the north, middle and south of the country. The northern journey began in Santiago de Compostela, went along the Atlantic coast and then, via a six-hour train journey from Bilbao, to the Mediterranean coast at Barcelona. The central portion took the shape of a loose arc around Madrid before heading east to the coast and Valencia. In the south, we began in Mallorca then crossed to Andalucía, following the coast before heading up to and ending in Seville.

These were personal journeys. Some were made with a film crew for the BBC series, some gardens we discovered en route and some Derry and I returned to in different seasons. There are doubtless gardens we should have visited and certainly others might have made a different selection. But the choice of gardens, the routes we took and our responses to each of them were always personal. It was an idiosyncratic, fascinating and rich experience, and I hope that we share that through the pages of this book.

Opposite: The Islamic rill running down the centre of the garden of Casa del Rey Moro in Ronda hints at a fictitious Moorish heritage.

Right: The garden of La Lancha near Jarandilla de la Vera in Extremadura is designed to deliberately blend in with an existing olive grove.

The baroque garden of Pazo de Oca is centred around two basins, both with islands as stylised boats. This, on the upper basin, is a symbol of Arcadian heaven, planted with fruit and flowers and a figure fishing in well-stocked waters.

Below: A balcony in the Casa de Pilatos in Seville, lined with a blaze of pelargoniums, provides essential shade from the Andalusian sun.

Opposite: Looking out onto the garden from the carefully restored Mudejar windows in the Palacio de Galiana just outside Toledo.

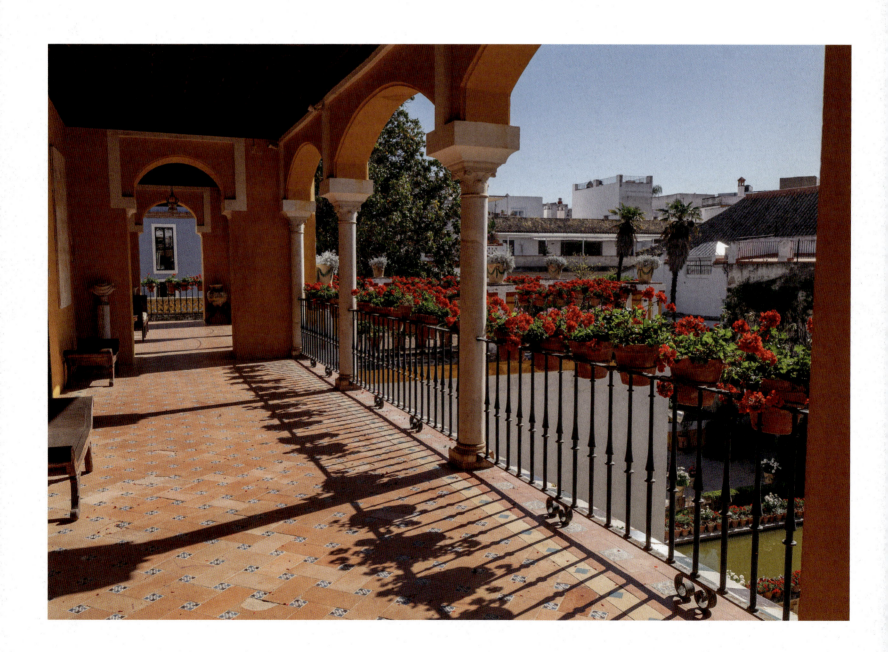

The grass entrance court of Pazo de Oca is flanked by the façade of the chapel dedicated to San Antonio de Padua. It was built between 1731 and 1752, replacing a former sixteenth-century hermitage.

Pazo de Oca
SANTIAGO DE COMPOSTELA

Driving south from Santiago, all is a rich green. On both sides of the road, as far as you can see, are tens of thousands of eucalypts in plantations, oaks and pines on the hillsides in the morning mist, meadows lush with grass, kiwi orchards strung on industrial-looking concrete pergolas covered with their vine-like foliage, fields of cabbages and potatoes just coming into flower and all suffused with a slightly damp, glistening green. Galicia on a misty midsummer morning is like Ireland or Pembrokeshire, the Spain of mountain and plain, searing summer heat and harshness far away in another world.

Derry and I were going to visit Pazo de Oca, barely 20 kilometres southwest of Santiago, deep in the Galician countryside. *Pazo* is the Galician word derived from 'palace', but that is not a fair description of Pazo de Oca. Pazo de Oca is often referred to as the 'Spanish Versailles' but it is nothing like Versailles – and all the better and more interesting for that. Whereas Versailles overloads on grandeur and size, but falls short on charm, Pazo de Oca has heft and style, but also a combination of charm and patrician status that is particular to this corner of Spain.

'Palace' implies stately grandeur, whereas this is a muscular mixture of castle, mansion and farm, set back on what looks like a village green bounded by estate houses (sold off long ago) and the lovely retained chapel. It is built out of a beautiful golden stone much weathered with lichen and moss.

There has been an establishment on the site since the thirteenth century, but the current building and baroque gardens are eighteenth century, with substantial additions and alterations made in the nineteenth and twentieth centuries. It belongs to the Dukes of Segorbe and the Casa Ducal de Medinaceli Foundation, who also own the famous Casa de Pilatos in Seville (page 263), with Pazo de Oca being used by them as a summer retreat from the extremes of Andalusian summers.

At the heart of the early eighteenth-century garden are two rectangular pools, slicing diagonally across the site, that were made by diverting two rivers so that they ran down into the garden and formed these pools, ponds, rills and fountains – as well as driving the mill for the estate's flour and serving the washhouse, with its large basin with sloping sides so the linen might be pounded and kneaded clean against the incline.

The ponds have walls crenellated by alternating stone balls and cones, sufficiently rough hewn to seem almost defensive rather than decorative. Blue hydrangeas hung down over the water in June, backed by 400-year-old box hedging grown into trees. There is box everywhere, clipped tight, fashioned into entrances and walls, and immaculately topiarised into a range of geometric shapes as well as grown into multi-stemmed trees.

The first pool, nearest the house and church and filled directly from water from the washhouse, symbolises a life spent obeying the laws of God and man, with a boat-shaped stone island filled with

Above: A doorway leading from the courtyard at the back of the house to the main gardens and ponds glows green in the cool, damp Galician summer.

Opposite: The two ponds are flanked by walls of local stone crenellated by alternating mossy stone balls and cones, which seem almost defensive rather than decorative.

flowers spilling from stone pots, citrus trees providing fruit and shade, and a statue of a contented man fishing in the fish-filled waters. This is not just the image of a perfect Arcadian Galician life but also of the Arcadian heaven that awaits the virtuous person.

A vine-arcaded crossing divides the two main pools, with the lower fed from the first with the water gushing down and out from a snake's head to the Pool of Vanity. Things have not gone so well in this lower section. The name is a clue as to the direction it takes you. It is occupied not by a delightful fishing boat but by a warship manned by monsters. This is the hell that awaits the loose-living, sinful man. However, for all the dire warnings that would certainly have been read loud and clear by all who visited, both portrayal of heaven and hell are utterly delightful; the two pools and their green surrounds blazoned with flower and white swans peacefully gliding on them convey a charm and lightness of touch that rather undermines the fierceness of the message.

Carry on across the dividing path and you come to the most dramatic remnant of the late

nineteenth-century changes to the garden. These were overseen by François de Vié to fit in with the fashion for a more romantic, looser, 'English' style. The main survivor of these changes is the avenue of lime trees flanking a box-hedged grass *allée* – too wide for a path, too soft-wearing for a driveway, and too long and directional for a lawn – leading to large wrought iron gates. Rising up to the left as you look down towards the gates at the far end is a grassy slope with new orchards, bounded by a distant high stone wall, and to the right, extensive new kitchen and rose gardens formally laid out in recent years within immaculately clipped box and yew hedges.

In amongst and interweaving are rills and rivulets and canals of water running down from the diverted rivers, the garden constantly backed by a soundtrack of moving water. This gives the whole place a kind of ornate intimacy, shapes and sounds repeating, developing and embellishing in layers, a horticultural green fugue.

The new vegetable and rose gardens are part of the substantial restoration and development that has taken place over the past 30 years. By the 1980s, the area they occupy had become a field with cattle grazing. The scale and ambition of this transformation is impressive and clearly very productive, though it lacks the worn, mossy-stoned charm of the older garden.

A new box maze has been laid out based upon the Fibonacci sequence and up nearer the house there is another existing maze based, somewhat surprisingly, upon a mosaic floor in Canterbury cathedral. A Galician *hórreo*, a wooden-sided long building, its purpose as a granary, raised up on substantial stone stilts to keep the rats and mice away, is also part of the garden, the horticultural and agricultural worlds overlapping and mingling with easy familiarity.

Should you visit in spring there would be a superb display of camellias, the Galician climate being ideal for them, but the layers of green, stone and water harmonising and blended by time and a particular strand of baroque lightness of touch is more than enough for me. Pazo de Oca in any season is a delight.

Left: The bridge dividing the two ponds is made from rough-hewn local stone.

Opposite: Two rivers were diverted to run into the garden to form ponds, rills and fountains – but this was not just decorative. The water first drove the mill wheel and passed through the washhouse with its large basin.

Overleaf: This avenue of lime trees flanking a box-hedged grass allée – leading to large wrought-iron gates – is the most visible remnant of nineteenth-century additions and changes to the garden.

Santiago de Compostela Allotments
SANTIAGO DE COMPOSTELA

THE ROAD TO SANTIAGO DE COMPOSTELA IS ONE WHICH HAS BEEN ENTHUSIASTICALLY ENDURED by over 300,000 pilgrims each year and many millions across the past thousand years. Whilst the motivation for what is always a long and arduous trek ranges across hundreds of variations, between a jolly good walk and a profound desire to atone for sins and purify the soul, the goal of the Camino remains the baroque facade of the cathedral in the Praza do Obradoiro, wherein once lay the mortal remains of St James the apostle. Well, sort of.

The story behind the pilgrimage is this: St James the apostle, brother of St John, introduced Christianity to Spain but, on his return to the Holy Land, had his head cut off for his pains by King Herod in AD 44. His corpse was then put into a boat by disciples and, despite the lack of sail or oars, it miraculously made its way through the Mediterranean and up the Iberian coast, until beached in Galicia near modern Padrón. The body was then taken inland and buried and forgotten about for 800 years. But it was then noticed that in the middle of the forest where the body lay, stars shone especially brightly – making a field of stars – and further investigations revealed the tomb of the unfortunate St James. So a church was built around the tomb which, despite various sackings and incarnations, became the cathedral to St James of the Field of Stars – Santiago de Compostela.

The timing of this coincided with Moorish retreat from Galicia and St James became a symbol of Christian resistance to Islam, wielding a sword in one hand and a cross in the other to rally troops to see off the heathen invaders. It is said that he appeared, always riding a white charger, at least 40 times in battles against the Moors, spurring the Spanish to victory and, despite being very Galician, becoming a symbol of an independent, unified Spain seeing off all unwanted foreigners. It is no coincidence that Franco, himself a proud Galician, was a great admirer of St James.

In any event, only Jerusalem and Rome have greater status as a destination for Christian pilgrimage. When you walk through the twenty-first-century streets on a warm June evening, you do so amongst a steady stream of weary pilgrims plodding uphill to their journey's end, staff in hand and scallop shell stitched to their clothes or backpacks. Scallop shells appear etched into the granite walls, pavements, stones and houses all along the route, right up to the square itself filled with tired but elated pilgrims, some reverential and evidently moved, others celebrating and many just delighted to have finished so they can stop at last.

There are a number of different theories as to why a scallop shell is so associated with the Camino but it seems probable that it originated as a badge that was picked from the beach at Fisterra (Finisterre) – the world's end – which, having paid all appropriate dues at Santiago de Compostela and recovered sufficient health and energy, was the pilgrim's final destination and the shell was sewn onto the pilgrim's hat or cloak to display that they had walked the walk. From the splayed grooves in the shell was taken the symbolism of the many different routes of the Camino converging in one centre.

In the medieval period, Santiago was full of gardens, both public and private, attached to the many hospitals and lodgings where pilgrims could recover from the notoriously arduous journey and, from 1350, after the Black Death had killed more than half of the Spanish population, be quarantined against potential plague.

I walked under the canopy of oaks in Parque de la Alameda on the hillside looking across at the cathedral and could see that if you had crossed the Pyrenees and arrived arduous weeks later via Burgos and Léon a bit of R & R in this soft, cool green shade would be deliciously restorative. But, having flown and driven into town, my own *camino* was limited to poking around the back streets looking to see what people were growing. Other than a few window boxes and the odd pot fixed to a wall, not a lot.

However, on one of the streets rising up to the cathedral square, I followed an elderly man clutching a pair of garden shears. There was something about the way he was holding them that indicated he intended to use them. He slipped down a narrow alley which opened out to become a grassy track with an overgrown area on one side and on the other, an allotment tucked in the heart of the city, hidden from all the pilgrim-thronged streets but with the facade of the cathedral rising above it.

Apparently, these allotment plots are distributed by the council free of charge to applicants for a period of four years, at the end of which they can reapply for another four-year term or allow someone else to have use of them.

The gentleman with shears began to cut the hedge surrounding his plot. It was full of brambles and weeds but had a large walnut tree in its centre. He said he was too old to look after it properly now but he collected the nuts and the blackberries. I asked about the overgrown areas on the other side of the track. They were plots, he said, and were used in the past, but the council didn't clear the nettles and brambles, and that's depressing. But he smiled sweetly and did not seem very depressed, cutting away vigorously.

His own, rather underplanted plot was on the very edge of the site that was filled with scores of well-tended plots with roses, raspberries, beans, courgettes, sweetcorn, garlic, lots of rosemary and sage and every kind of salad leaf. A couple of big fig trees cast a deep shade. Perhaps a dozen people were gently but intently moving around, carefully gathering or tending in the evening light. The atmosphere was collective, as though a group had all agreed to come as one and share a few jobs and harvest, with none of the competitive horticultural intensity you can sometimes find on British allotments.

Watching them for a while, I noticed that people would select flowers or produce from more than one plot, gathering a few leaves here, some beans there, maybe pick a rose or two. I then noticed that everyone seemed to be collecting the same mixture of plants – each bundle was slightly different but all of a kind. A pair of men, perhaps in their thirties, were gathering handfuls of herbs and flowers in

bouquets, which turned out to be part of a longstanding Galician tradition of hanging fragrant herbs above the door on St John's Eve – 23 June – that commemorates the birth of John the Baptist and midsummer. They told me that they also made a decoction of the herbs, steeping them overnight and then using the water to wash with in the morning. I saw that they had rosemary, fennel, lemon verbena, sage, lavender, rue and artemisia, all particular to this Galician midsummer ritual.

There is a quote from Thomas Hardy saying that you can always tell a genuine rural tradition from one that has been revived because the former will always have a kind of unselfconscious truculence about it, whilst the revived dance, song or whatever it may be is performed with extra enthusiasm. So the easy, low-key matter-of-factness of these two relatively young men, wandering from allotment to allotment plot, chatting, gathering ingredients for an ancient conflation of Christian and pagan ritual, was striking, the whole process being played out in much the same way as if they were gathering salad leaves for dinner. It seemed that most of the plots were growing ingredients, whether floral, herbal or vegetable, for local Galician dishes, treatments and ceremonies with the same easy aplomb and connection to season and place that has all but disappeared in twenty-first-century Britain.

Although the allotment site had the backdrop of the rather grand council offices, and the towers of the cathedral up above it and the square, still packed with arriving pilgrims and tourists, was an easy stone's throw away, this was an inner world of Santiago, not tucked away or pushed to one side but in the middle of all the paraphernalia of the Camino and one of the most visited Christian sites in the world. All that passed by outside this little haven of local people going about their daily lives.

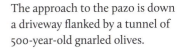
The approach to the pazo is down a driveway flanked by a tunnel of 500-year-old gnarled olives.

Pazo Santa Cruz de Rivadulla
SANTIAGO DE COMPOSTELA

A FEW KILOMETRES NORTH OF PAZO DE OCA IS THE MORE OBVIOUSLY AGRICULTURAL ESTATE OF Pazo Santa Cruz De Rivadulla. Not only is the house enclosed by arable land but it also has the largest camellia nursery in Spain, offering over 500 different varieties – and for good camellia measure, the garden has the oldest camellia trees in Spain.

But I confess that I am largely immune to the charms of camellias. However, I was spared the complications of insincere appreciation because they had all long since finished flowering by the time of my midsummer visit. But it took no empty niceties to admire the magnificent olive avenue leading up to the house and garden, which I would not trade for a million camellias in full bloom. It has been there since the family took possession of the pazo 500 years ago and is now a long, gnarled tunnel filtering glaucous light and a cobwebbed tracery of shade to the ground. It is bounded by a patchwork of small square fields bounded by olives with side avenues leading to the nursery, hidden away in the woods. A vegetable plot, clearly for the household but almost on an agricultural scale, is full of beans, Padrón peppers, potatoes and kale. The layout, with fields, woodland and garden all integrated and contained within a stone boundary wall, remains as originally set out in the sixteenth century.

The current owner, Juan Armada Díez de Rivera, tenth Marqués de Rivadulla, met me with children, grandchildren and friends all in attendance, bikes parked by the front door, children dodging and playing, the sense of family life running through every stone and plant of the place.

The farm buildings are beautiful, flowing in an unbroken series of yards to the chapel and house via barns, winery, a long *hórreo* on solid capped legs, threshing yard, reservoir and indeterminate low buildings all uniformly roofed with wave upon wave of terracotta tiles.

The garden is at the back of the house, with a large formal area laid out as symmetrical, box-edged flower beds with roses, dahlias and bearded irises, seemingly grown for cutting or as specimens rather than to create a mixed border of any kind, and fronted by a mass of gardenias planted in a grid grown to provide cut flowers for the house. Down its full length is a vine-covered pergola made from granite columns of exceptional height because it was originally the entrance and had to be tall enough to accommodate horses and riders. Oranges, palms and ferns flank the path that leads through to a wooded area, although that undersells its provenance. It is really a superb collection of trees, an arboretum. Many were planted at the end of the nineteenth century by Iván Armada, the seventh marquis, who introduced nearly 5,000 specimens to the garden, many of which are still remaining and now exceptionally large, including giant magnolias, multi-stemmed Dicksonia ferns on a scale normally only possible to see in New Zealand or Tasmania, and a huge *Phytolacca dioica*, or ombú, from Argentina, its elephantine trunk looking as though it was bubbling out of the ground as a result of much coppicing.

Juan Armada clearly adores his trees – and in particular camellias – and refers to them all as individuals, each with their own story, and has known them all his life. But he is unsentimental about them. They lost a huge palm the previous winter but he shrugs at this. 'Trees have a life. They live and then they die.'

We walk uphill though giant box trees, planted in the seventeenth century, probably as hedging or for topiary, but now the multi-stemmed trunks are sinuous and quite bare, and the small leaves just spangles of green high up against the blue sky. A square pond, made to feed the mill that is further down the hillside, is made cool and dark by the shade of surrounding tulip trees. I go down to see the waterfall but now, in midsummer, it is a modest flow. However, in winter, it apparently roars and bounces angrily down the hillside. Galicia is a very wet place, although they rarely get a frost and Juan says that it has definitely got milder in his lifetime.

Rivadulla has remained in the same family since 1510 and the passion for plants has been handed down through the generations. But with the climate changing, I cannot help but wonder how the garden, so established and so evolved for the Galician damp, mild climate, will change too.

A pergola made from local granite carries vines harvested for wine. It was built in the eighteenth century and became the main approach to the house, made exceptionally high to allow enough room for horse and rider to pass beneath it.

El Abeo
RIBADESELLA

THIS IS THE STORY OF A GARDEN THAT CHANGED ITS ADDRESS. THE HOUSE WAS BUILT IN 1691 on the north Atlantic coast of Asturias as a large but not ostentatiously grand manor house in the local style. Over the centuries, the family lived in it contentedly, both as a main home and as their country retreat from Madrid. But after the Second World War, a coal mine was developed nearby and its tunnelling began to undermine the house. Despite the catastrophic implications of this, the Argüelles family did not want to leave the house, so they did the next best thing – they decided that the house itself should leave. So in 1968, they began the process of moving the entire house and much of the garden, stone by stone, brick by brick, plant by plant, to its current position 16 kilometres away, in the tiny hamlet of Abeo, a mile or so inland from the coast, near the resort town of Ribadesella, where people from Madrid have holiday homes where they can enjoy the coolness of summer and the mildness of winter.

Whilst not all the garden could be transported, an astonishing amount was, including the beautifully clipped large box hedging that flanks the drive, the arched stone entrance gate, the chapel, stone walls, the *hórreo* with its subtle Asturian styling differentiating it from a Galician version, a fountain, statues and even the cobbles of the entrance yard.

Apparently, it took a while to settle upon this new location for the house because, as Marta Argüelles told me, her grandfather insisted on going somewhere completely quiet. The bar for this was set high. A number of other potential sites, noticeably silent, were rejected. But then he came here and sat silently in a chair for a day, and decided that it was the ideal location. The sea lay soundlessly before it and behind the house was an uninterrupted view out to the Picos mountains in the silent distance.

Left: The front of the house faces towards the sea and the view from the back looks out to the distant mountains of the Asturian interior.

Opposite: The garden has a lushness and intensity of green only found in this northwestern corner of Spain.

Overleaf: The formal pond was created after the house was moved but the building, down to the last tile, was moved 16 kilometres to its new home and rebuilt exactly as it had been before.

The result is a curious mixture of the deep-rooted establishment of an old house and the freshness of the new. The charcoal paintwork gleams, roof tiles are unweathered and there is a crispness to all the edges. However, the Asturian climate, with its mildness and abundance of rain in all seasons, means that the garden is exuberantly green and, for all the evident attention and work given by the three gardeners to cutting the hedges, mowing the grass and edging the paths, there is a pleasant fuzziness of unstoppable growth wherever you look.

In front of the house, across the cobbled courtyard with the chapel at one end, you go down steps to a long rectangular lily pond tightly bounded by box hedging. Behind it is a disproportionately tall cypress hedge. Apparently, this was once arcaded to allow selective views of the sea, but they also allowed selective views of the house and garden from the road and the desire for privacy overcame the virtues of a sea view and the arcades were allowed to grow over.

To one side of the driveway, behind one of the transported box hedges, is an area of trees and shrubs set in grass, with some magnificent tree ferns, adding an unexpected exotic note and clearly happy in the benign mildness of the climate. A pair of holm oaks grow side by side, oak twins, planted here having been brought to the garden as acorns gathered in Dublin, where a member of the family was the Spanish ambassador.

The garden behind the house is dominated by a large lawn with a stone fountain relocated along with the house. The lawn is billiard-baize green and as perfectly flat and immaculately tended – the impossible dream of any garden south of this lush, northern fringe of Asturias, Galicia, Cantabria and the Basque Country. Borders with flowering shrubs attend at the edges, but like supplicants to the grass, not the main event.

The lawn leads to a balustrade that looks down onto another long lily pond fed from water that cascades from the retaining end wall. Beyond this, the ground slopes away through mass planting of trees into the haziness of the cloud merging into the mountains.

I was taken to an area of borders filled with roses and edged by broad box hedges with a marvellous

Above: In front of and below the entrance courtyard, perfectly clipped box hedges contain a lily pond and a high Leyland cypress hedge screens the house from the road.

Left: A collection of tree ferns thrive in the damp, mild climate of Asturias.

Right: A view across the garden to the mountains beyond from inside the house.

panera – a larger, balconied version of the Galician *hórreo*, raised up on higher stone legs relocated along with everything else – stretching across one end. This had been the vegetable garden and, as well as the roses, contained large herbaceous borders. This, it was made clear, was exceptional and a source of great pride. Herbaceous plants are almost impossible to find in Spain because no one grows them and it is only here, in Asturias, where the climate is mild and damp enough, that, if you can source them, they can flourish. It was a strange experience, admiring a herbaceous border like a million others growing in a million British gardens. I thought of the tree ferns flourishing over on the other side of the house, so tall and lush, and the ones in my own garden I have to protect from winter cold and summer drought. Everything is exotic to someone, and all our treasured exotica commonplace to others.

Faculty buildings of the University of Cantabria flank one side of the wildlife reserve of Vaguada de Las Llamas that has been created from a site filled with building and industrial waste.

Vaguada de Las Llamas
SANTANDER

TAKING THE ROAD TO SANTANDER, THE ASTURIAN AND THEN CANTABRIAN LANDSCAPE IS DRESSED with the midsummer-green canopy of seemingly endless oak trees covering the waves of hills that rise from the coast up towards the Picos mountains and national park.

Santander is a stop-off on the road to Bilbao, to visit the newly landscaped Vaguada de Las Llamas. 'Las Llamas' refers to the long marshy strip of wetlands running in from the coast that dominates the 11-hectare (27-acre) site on the north side of the city, overlooked by the University of Cantabria on one side and new blocks of housing on the other.

The marshland had become a waste ground with the drainage hindered by dumped building rubble and the marsh polluted by urban wastewater. But at the beginning of this century, the city bought the land from private industrial owners and commissioned a park. From the outset, the park had three clear goals: to provide recreational space for the city, to have buildings and sites for cultural events and to create a nature reserve – and that all these three functions should coexist without compromise. On top of this, with climate change increasingly bringing extreme periods of wet weather, the marshland was important to absorb water that would otherwise be channelled by hard landscaping to create flooding.

Work began in 2006 and the first phase was opened a year later. Now, nearly two decades on, it has evolved to become a remarkably successful prototype of urban regeneration of lost landscapes that can provide access to sports and play areas and to wildlife without impinging on either the quality of the human recreation or the ecosystem as a whole.

The buildings are modern and bold, the planting confident. There has been no attempt to blend the styles of the different areas and yet there is no absolute demarcation. At the end nearest the sea, hard by a football stadium, is a huge, curved, silver concert hall planted with trees and grass that then leads down via stylised terracing to a pond, and from there to wetlands filled with reeds that dominate the central area. The imposition of a starkly modern building and its ancillary landscape, including a car park and picnicking area, flows easily and eventually seamlessly into the nature reserve where wooden walkways traverse down in amongst the reeds, meaning you can look down on the birds and dragonflies skirting and skating the water's surface and, should you be lucky, the otters that are also there.

The slopes are wooded and the grass beneath trees uncut, all increasing the diversity of habitats and therefore species. The wetlands have proved particularly popular with migratory birds, who use them as a stopping-off point on the journey north and south.

All this in the centre of a busy city makes Vaguada de Las Llamas an exemplar of how to incorporate the seemingly conflicting demands of people, wildlife and environmental factors, showing that it is possible to create modern urban spaces without compromising on the quality of any of the three elements.

Left: Areas of clear water flow into an expanse of reeds, providing the perfect environment for a wide range of aquatic life.

Opposite: The great success of the park is that it combines the demands and virtues of an urban park for recreation, a haven for wildlife and a meaningful contribution to counter the effects of climate change.

Jeff Koons' *Puppy* is a giant floral terrier inspiring delight and disdain in equal measure – but never indifference.

The Floral Puppy

BILBAO

Is it a sculpture? Yes, certainly. Is it a garden? No, not really. Yet perhaps no less a garden than a 'green wall' or any other form of vertical planting that the horticultural world enthusiastically embraces. Jeff Koons' *Puppy* sculpture of a huge West Highland terrier sitting guard outside the Guggenheim Museum in central Bilbao is likely to enrage or delight according to age and disposition, but this particular old codger found it entertaining, dramatic and delightful.

Just like a hanging basket, a window box or any large pot, it is a display of growing plants – 38,000 of them – changed seasonally, watered, weeded and nurtured to look as good as possible. Birds nest in amongst them and insects feed on the nectar. It is a form of topiary insomuch that the shape is defined by living plants and it is fun and creative. If it is not your idea of what a garden ought to be then that is fine. Sit back and enjoy the ride.

Frank Gehry's Guggenheim building arouses equally divided responses. There are those who see it as a flashy trifle (albeit a hugely expensive one; in all it cost the Bilbao government over 180 million dollars) that detracts from the substance of one of Spain's great cities and those who love its innovation and chutzpah in making the structure of the gallery a fascinating piece of art in itself. I belong wholeheartedly to the second camp. I find it a wonderfully inspiring piece of architecture and believe Bilbao is greatly enhanced by its presence.

It was built in the 1990s in the port area by the Nervión River, once the hub of Bilbao's heavy industrial trade – which in turn was the centre of heavy industry in Spain, but, like so many industrial centres in cities, became abandoned as the industries declined in the 1970s and 1980s, with over 60,000 manufacturing jobs lost in the city in the 20 years between 1975 and 1995. But since its opening in 1997, the gallery is reckoned to have brought in over 700,000 new visitors a year to this part of Bilbao.

Jeff Koons' floral West Highland terrier cannot be regarded separately from Frank Gehry's building, although in fact it was created before the building began. It was originally made in 1992 for a German exhibition, was reassembled in Sydney, then bought by the Guggenheim foundation in 1997 and brought to Bilbao to stand in front of the newly built gallery. The gallery and sculpture dominate this part of Bilbao, with trams running along tree-lined tracks set in grass below it and an energy restored to what could have been just another remnant of lost industry.

Photographs tend to obscure the size of the puppy. It is enormous, the size of a building, commanding the space around it. Because Gehry's building is itself so sculptural, the scale and the bright, not to say kitsch, colours of the 12-metre-high dog hold their own and are not cowed by the flowing titanium, glass and limestone walls behind it.

In summer, it is planted with petunias, calendulas, begonias and verbena. Then, in autumn, all these are removed and replaced with 38,000 violas and pansies. Variegated ivy grows under the shade of the chin. The body is made of steel, with an outer wall half a metre deep filled with compost and covered with an absorbent landscape fabric containing 38,000 holes to accommodate the roots of the plants. The replanting involves completely scaffolding the sculpture and takes a team of 20 people 10 days to do. Despite all this palaver, this is just a form of bedding, still solemnly played out in scores of parks and council sites by people who would decry the puppy as not 'real' gardening.

A door in the puppy's nether regions opens to reveal a gleaming silver interior, more akin to a spaceship than canine anatomy, with a network of silver pipes and sprinklers controlled by computers. All this contrasts with the ephemerality of flowers and the pop culture of Koons' work – which is perhaps a way of saying that for all the seeming superficiality of the piece, this is a serious piece of art, built to last.

The site of Frank Gehry's Guggenheim building in the old port area of the Nervión River was once the heart of Spain's heavy industry and has been a huge factor in regenerating Bilbao.

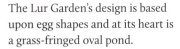
The Lur Garden's design is based upon egg shapes and at its heart is a grass-fringed oval pond.

Lur Garden
SAN SEBASTIÁN

IT IS LESS THAN TEN KILOMETRES FROM THE CENTRE OF SAN SEBASTIÁN TO THE LUR GARDEN in Oiartzun as the crow flies, but for the earthbound traveller the roads get smaller and twistier in the Basque countryside, the overhanging trees get greener and damper, and the mist deepens until it feels as though even finding the garden will be a feat. The Basque language on the signposts is impenetrably remote from any idea of other European languages and adds to the sense of entering another dimension.

But the instructions proved to be accurate, leading me to the entrance which is a cobbled path crossing a stream edged by huge fern fronds, before going through a gate in old railings. Banana leaves glimpsed through the trees suggest more than just lush Basque verdancy and the path duly becomes flanked by an army of ensete bananas, their huge leaves tinged with ruby and chocolate. The trunks of dead or felled trees, mostly robinias, serve as ornamental posts and supports for climbing plants, sunk in the borders by the dozen amongst large, clipped boulders of yew. Grasses, coleus and begonias jostle and mingle. The planting is wild and rich and full-on from the outset. This is not so much a mood setter as an immersion into a horticultural cold shower to wake you up, get you on top of your game, because any visit to the Lur Garden is going to be a wild and wonderful ride.

The garden belongs to the Spanish garden designer and television host Iñigo Segurola Arregui, and every element of it has been made by him from a meadow that, when he arrived, was still grazed by sheep. It was conceived out of despair but has come to fulfilment as an expression of triumphant hope. Iñigo and his then husband set up their design practice in the building looking out onto the garden, which is all glass walls, green roof and hundreds of cacti and succulents in pots in tiers in front of the building, and inside a cool – in every sense of the word – studio has a handful of young people at work.

The garden is two hectares (five acres) in size and set in an amphitheatre in the woods flanked by trees, the rest of the world unseen and practically unheard. It is a secret space that Iñigo has created, planted and tends almost entirely single-handed, and which he occupies as a force of nature. He is a broad-shouldered, barrel-chested pirate of a man, living and gardening alone but, like the garden, dramatically filling a big space. He also has three superb golden retrievers which of course endears him to me for life.

The idea or concept behind the design came in 2012 in the middle of a sleepless night. This moment of inspiration was simple enough: the garden should be egg-shaped. All of it. He got up and drew out the design before dawn and then spent years making that a reality, the process saving him from a deep depression as his marriage fell apart.

At the centre of the garden is a large oval grass area with 16 inner ovals of long meadow grass linked by mown paths. The grass is the natural meadow grass that was on the site when he came. He cuts it once a year at Christmas and gradually wildflowers are finding their way in. To one side, backed by the hedge dividing it from the next garden, is a large bed dominated by hundreds of pink and white cleome amongst cardoons, agapanthus, echinacea and clipped yew eggs. It is apparent that when Iñigo likes something he likes it a lot and goes for it in a big way.

The next area, the mirror garden, is based around an oval pond, the water black and exactly level with the surrounding tightly mown grass. All three dogs leapt in and the mirror of the water was shattered by canine aquabatics. On one side is a huge, curved mixed border filled with plants in every shade of yellow – with rudbeckia, tagetes, phlomis, hypericum, coleus 'Golden Bedder', day lilies – and the deep purple of ricinus, ensete and cannas. Tree-sized tetrapanax provide height and a little shade. The other side of this mirror garden has a sweep of weeping swamp cypresses supported from spilling and spooling down to and along the ground by a scaffolding of more dead tree trunks.

A big-leaf garden lies beyond this, leading to a pink and red garden with more tetrapanax, colocasia, bergenias, filipendula, canna 'Australia', pink hydrangeas and lots of cosmos. All the separate spaces are defined by beech hedges, all rounded, as wide as they are high, planted in sinuous curves. The entire garden seems to be without any kind of straight line or edge.

The garden is bounded by a stream along one side and within the cool humidity of its banks are scores of Dicksonias in various stages of growth. Iñigo told me they grow eight centimetres a year here and most have been raised by him from self-sown seedlings.

This takes you into the hydrangea maze with, when I was there in late June, seemingly hundreds of them – *Hydrangea quercifolia*, *H. villosa*, *H. paniculata* and, above all, 'Annabelle', billowing clouds of rich mauve, pink and white flowers. Sooner or later, if you visit enough gardens, you see what a certain group of plants are really like, what they can aspire to be and attain, given the right conditions. In that respect, the Lur Garden is the epicentre of hydrangea heaven. The soil is very sandy and stony so drains well. If they occasionally get a frost it is only a degree or so; they have at least a metre of rain and it is warm and very humid in summer. This, exactly this, is what hydrangeas like best.

Above: The garden grows in a valley tucked deep into the heavily wooded Basque countryside.

Overleaf: The garden is bounded by a stream along one side and within the cool humidity of its banks are stone cushions topped with moss and scores of Dicksonia tree ferns, mostly raised from self-sown seedlings and growing rampantly in the mild humidity.

What I liked best in this garden that is so packed with plants and so exuberant in style and sustained energy was the Moon Garden. Iñigo bought a mass of huge flat stones on a whim and he said that they lay unused for a few years because although he liked them, he didn't know what to do with them. Then he got a digger in and, in a morning, laid them out, without a plan, just directing stone after stone as the sequence presented itself to his eye.

The result is a masterpiece. These great slabs are laid on raised soil berms like sections of a giant path or geological sandstone pavement, with grikes and clints filled with spilling white and silver flowers and grasses – pennisetum, *Miscanthus sinensis*, gaura, *Ammi visnaga*, candytufts and everywhere white erigeron. Topiarised yew eggs add structure to the borders and, as with the whole garden, everywhere you look there is the rising backdrop of trees from the valley sides.

It is a spectacular place, with a lot of everything, overflowing with plants and concepts and its own kinetic energy. It is almost overwhelming, almost too much, but actually a horticultural feast, and you leave full to the brim but delighted and privileged to have taken part in this gardening *grande bouffe*.

Left: The garden is the creation of the Spanish garden designer Iñigo Segurola Arregui.

Below: Iñigo's design studio was the first thing to be built on the site – which was then a meadow grazed by sheep.

Opposite: Outside the low, grass-roofed studio building are scores of terracotta pots filled with cacti and succulents arranged like found objects and sculpture rather than a plant collection.

The famous zinc dragon and umbrella outside Casa Bruno Cuadros on Las Ramblas, which was once an umbrella shop.

Las Ramblas
BARCELONA

It is a long train ride from Bilbao to Barcelona. You skirt the foothills of the Pyrenees for a few hours before the countryside becomes flatter, drier, harder at the edges, with unbounded fields dominated by wheat and wine, a rolling agricultural Aragonese and Catalan landscape following the contours on a scale unimaginable in Galicia or Asturias, let alone anywhere in Britain.

Six hours after leaving Bilbao-Abando station, we arrived in Barcelona in the dark, the humid streets hotter at midnight than midday in Bilbao. In the night, the heat broke and thunder, lightning and heavy rain lashed my hotel window. By morning, the air had been cleansed and I was up early to visit Las Ramblas before the crowds descended – and descend they do, in multitudes, starting with locals heading to work first thing and, a little more gradually, tourists flocking in to tick off an essential part of the full Barcelona experience.

The Ramblas run from Plaça de Catalunya and were created from a stream that ran through the city down to the port; when it dried up in summer it was used as a track. In the eighteenth century, the stream was diverted, the Ramblas paved and trees planted. It became a place to promenade and shop, but also a meeting place for friends, lovers and crowds. It was where Picasso would drink when he lived in Barcelona and where Orwell watched barricades being built during the Civil War.

However, at seven in the morning, after the previous night's storm, the streets were slightly steamy, still a little wet, and the light soupy. The buildings are painted ice cream colours – strawberry, pistachio, pale coffee – and the long avenue of palms, planes and lime trees was occupied mostly by street people and rough sleepers using the fountains to wash in.

Gradually, the earliest workers emerged from the subway and slowly the café chairs were taken off the tables, the stalls uncovered and the coffee machines turned on. Disappointingly, I did not find

the pet stalls where, according to Jan Morris in her book *Spain,* 'you may buy anything from a mouse to a monkey'.

Everyone, without exception, was either in shorts, a summer dress or just a shirt. This assumption of warm, rain-free weather was something of a culture shock, coming as I had the day before from the north of the country, where the wetness and coolness are both unavoidable and the reason why people come from the south – and perhaps Catalonia. The enormity of Spain and the differences between the regions always leaps out at you. Independence is for many Catalans and Basques a greater bond than their mutual Spanish identity.

The flower stalls opened up and the displays stacked outside – all bright colours with orchids, lilies, begonias, chrysanthemums, sunflowers and roses. These are flowers for displaying indoors and their provenance and connection to gardens is clearly of no concern – but they are popular and people are buying. I spoke to Carolina, whose family has run the same stall in the same spot here on the Ramblas for four generations. She said that people loved to buy flowers, no matter what time of year. Flowers made people happy.

The work traffic thins and the tourists start to take over, settling for *cafés con leche* and pastries in bars, taking selfies and, in their own way, promenading, using the Ramblas as intended, as they have always been used.

Left: One of the features of Las Ramblas are the flower stalls, some of which have been there, run by the same family, for generations.

Opposite: The plane trees lean in over the boulevard to provide shade for both tourists, who make a beeline for the street, and the locals. This was once the course of a stream and takes its name from the Catalan for a dry river bed or wadi.

Opposite: The vegetable garden at Pedralbes is based upon documents discovered in the archives with detailed accounts of pre-Columbian growing and dietary regimes, creating a fascinating living archive.

Overleaf: The fourteenth-century cloisters surround a garden with herbs and a medieval cistern as well as modern cypresses.

Pedralbes Monastery
BARCELONA

WHEN THE MONASTERY OF PEDRALBES WAS FIRST BUILT IN THE EARLY FOURTEENTH CENTURY, it was on a gentle hillside near the city. It is now firmly set in an affluent northern suburb of Barcelona, home of footballers, tennis players and lawyers, the high gates, large houses and sunshine having something of California about them. The monastery was destined for the order of the Poor Clares, who still have nuns living there. I had come across the order many years ago when I nearly sold my large but rickety house on a Herefordshire hillside to them, but it proved too rickety or perhaps not large enough. In any event, the huge Pedralbes monastery, despite a long and turbulent history that involved occupation by Napoleon's troops, the confiscation of church property in the mid-nineteenth century and the inevitable deterioration of the buildings, is beautifully restored and maintained.

The three-tiered main cloister has a water tank within a tiled enclosure which itself sits under the shade of a circle of large cypresses, dwarfing the accompanying planting of orange trees. Beds of irises and herbs line one side. The cloisters are cool and beautiful, and the garden adds a softness and greenness to the building, but this was not why I was here. What is more interesting horticulturally was to be found down some stairs on the next, lower level, further down the slope.

At the base of the buildings is a walled area that was used as a vegetable and physic garden for the nuns, which, like every medieval monastic foundation, would have been self-sufficient in medicinal herbs and grown as much of their own food as possible.

By the end of the twentieth century, this garden had become completely abandoned. But in 2017, it was decided to recreate the pre-Columbian monastic garden based upon fourteenth- and fifteenth-century Catalan manuscripts that had been found in the monastery archives. This meant that not

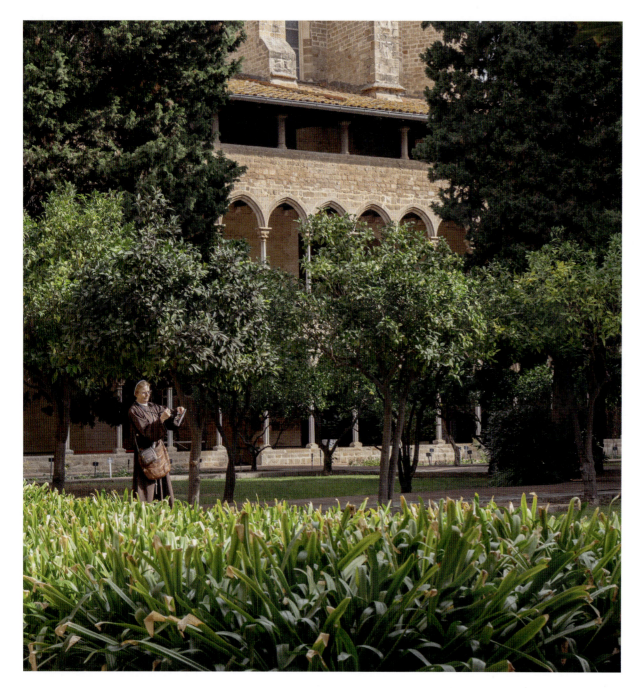

Orange and lemon trees grow in the cloister and a new orchard has been planted next to the restored vegetable garden replicating the fifteenth-century layout.

only would it recreate this particular garden but also be relevant to monastic gardens across Europe in a particular moment in time, between 1327, when Pedralbes monastery was founded, and Columbus's expedition in 1492 – which also was the beginning of the era of post-Islamic Spain. In every way a new world. The cut-off date meant that there could be no plants introduced from the Americas. So no tomatoes, potatoes, green beans. No sweetcorn, chillies, pumpkins or squashes and courgettes, let alone flowering plants like dahlias, sunflowers, asters, lupins and other American flowers that have since become the mainstay of European gardens.

As well as using the appropriate plants for the pre-Columbian exchange, the restoration of the gardens has also faithfully followed the medieval cultivation and irrigation techniques and layout. No machinery is used and the tools replicate those of the medieval period – not that these have changed much in the intervening 500 years.

The garden is divided into two plots, the second of which is intended primarily for fruit. It was just opened when I visited for the second time in spring 2024 and looked, frankly, raw and bare. Time will furnish it. The other plot, which is fully in use, has two sections divided by a wide path. Both are subdivided into small, temporary raised beds reached by narrow straw-covered paths. The straw is golden and appetisingly clean, a far cry from the mud-blotted straw paths I once used in my own northern, much wetter, garden.

The dryness of the climate and the need for careful water management was as pressing 500 years ago as now. Rainwater from the cloister roofs is collected in a large cistern, built in 1495. Then, by opening a sluice by turning a large, gleamingly modern brushed steel wheel, it runs along a brick channel that has openings at regular intervals. Simple wooden sluices, lifted as and when needed by hand, mean the water can be diverted into four ditches – each dug as temporary trenches. The water is then directed to each of the small raised beds by damming the main ditch, done by blocking it with soil heaped up with a mattock, so the flow moves sideways and encircles the raised bed like a moat. Then, when it is sufficiently soaked, the earth dam is broken down again by the mattock and the ditch re-established. The water moves on to the next bed and the process is repeated. When all the beds in the row have been irrigated, the delivery ditch – one of the four – is dammed by pushing the wooden shutter back down into place and so it moves along.

It is a beautifully simple and surprisingly beautiful process.

As well as individual crops growing in each of the beds, the researchers found recipes and records of specific combinations of vegetables that were grown, cooked and eaten in different seasons. So one bed has rocket (arugula), flat-leaf parsley and a local variety of very peppery cress. These plants were always grown by broadcasting the seed as a mixture and then harvested together to be eaten raw as a salad. Another bed contains a similar broadcast mixture consisting of chard, spinach and garlic – these would have been gathered, cooked in one pot and eaten as a hot dish in colder weather.

There are also methods of pest control documented, such as under-sowing brassica crops with clover to deter cabbage white butterflies, the clover also improving fertility by 'fixing' nitrogen from their air into the soil, which the brassica crops would then use.

Many of the beds had herbs and plants that we would consider border flowers – like aquilegias, achillea and alchemilla – all of which were used medicinally to make decoctions, unguents and teas to treat a wide range of ailments, as recorded in the found manuscripts.

The garden is intended as a living museum and encourages local schools and adults to join in the many workshops it runs. It is a superb example of bringing history and modern gardening, food and medicine together, making connections that the fifteenth-century nuns would have thought absurd to even question but which most modern children are barely aware of.

Eight tiers of concrete planters form permanent green bands of planting incorporated into the structure of this commercial building to create what was a radical experiment when it was built in the 1970s.

The Planeta Building

BARCELONA

As the Avinguda Diagonal and Gran Via de Carles III converge, the busy multi-laned roads go under and over each other, and the buildings rise and strut with the architectural bluster that corporate HQs somehow seem to uniquely muster. But one building stands out through its appearance and history. This is the Planeta Building, originally built for Banca Catalana in the 1970s, when wholesale development was using up much of Barcelona's green spaces. To counter this, the architects incorporated planting into the exterior of the building on a scale that had never been seen before and which is still exceptional, making the Planeta one of the earliest examples of a 'green' building.

There are nearly four kilometres of plants in eight tiers in a belt around all the faces of the four interconnected octagonal blocks that make up the building. There are two levels of planters on each of the floors – the lower for trailing plants mainly viewed from outside the building and an upper one for more vertical plants that are visible from the road yet best seen and appreciated from inside. In all, there are over 12,000 plants and 46 different species.

Although the interior building was refurbished in 2022, the exterior has been left unaltered for the past 50 years and the original planting of pittisporum, atriplex, cotoneaster, trailing asparagus and ivy remains mostly the same. It is still dramatic and show-stopping after all these years, the rows of planting dripping down in a way that is integrated into the building, defining rather than adorning it.

From the inside, when sitting in the predictably anonymous open-plan offices of the publishing group Planeta, the view is fringed with green, filtering the light and providing shade. It is civilising and practical, cutting down on the need for air-conditioning and reducing energy consumption.

Maintaining the planting involves the gardeners kitting themselves out like a cross between

Special Forces and mountaineers before taking to the metal walkway that goes between the building and the planters. They clip themselves onto the safety wire running round at each level with a carabiner before whipping out secateurs from their holster and doing a spot of pruning. It is very macho and impressive but little real maintenance is needed. The plants are chosen for their hardiness and seem very happy, although some of the more exposed aspects are a little thin.

Down on the ground, the entrance has a kind of enthusiasm that lifts it above the drearily familiar corporate planting. It is a building that is proud of itself and its green credentials and wants to share that. So lots of squat sago palms (*Cycas revoluta*), the native Spanish chamaerops, towering date palms, kentias and ivy festooning down almost to the ground from the first-floor planters all work hard to endorse the greenness and commitment to the ethos of the building. This is a trait that keeps coming through in urban projects in Spain that are dedicated to improving the environment and dealing with the problems of climate change: when the commitment is made it is pursued with a vigour that puts many similar UK projects to shame. And it has endured: having started out as a radical experiment, the Planeta Building is now revered as the inspiration and prototype of much environmentally sensitive building that has followed in its wake all across the world.

Left: Multiple shoots from a hard-pruned cabbage palm, *Cordyline australis*, are part of the inspired and dramatic planting on the ground.

Opposite: Each planting band has two sections, an outer one with plants that are inclined to trail and thus look best from outside the building and an inner one with more upright planting best seen from inside.

Barcelona Botanical Garden
BARCELONA

The Barcelona Botanical Garden sits on the Montjuïc hillside in the centre of the oldest part of the city, the port behind it, looking inland to the remnants of the 1992 Olympic Village and the Palau Nacional where the 1929 International Exhibition was based. That exhibition and the Olympics transformed Barcelona, both physically and giving a huge boost to its tourism.

The Botanical Garden is a beneficiary of these dramatic changes, although it is not the first botanic garden on the hillside. In 1930, following the Great Exhibition, the Historic Botanical Garden was established on the site of two quarries on Montjuïc and officially opened in 1941. It was closed in 1986 due to the building of the infrastructure needed for the 1992 games, then reopened in 2003.

However, another, new, Botanical Garden was created from scratch after the Olympic games had finished and opened in 1999. It covers 14 hectares (35 acres) and consists of over 2,000 species of Mediterranean plants – which of course does not mean plants solely from around the Mediterranean sea but selected from the regions of the world classified as having a Mediterranean climate, which includes Australia, South Africa, Chile and California, as well as the Mediterranean basin. Each different region has its own patch of hillside, with the Canaries and Australia lowest down and North Africa, California and Chile nearest the top. They are set in grids created by overlapping triangles defined by paths on the hillside, so the triangles stretch and veer to accommodate the slope. Even over short elevations, the planting shows the effect of altitude as they rise.

My first visit was on a July afternoon, when it was scorching and the hillside was parched. By definition, Mediterranean plants have to cope with extreme heat and drought in summer and they were certainly all getting their full dose of that. But a subsequent visit the following April

revealed a transformation. The previously stripped back and blasted hillside was alive with flowers and richly covered in green.

The entrance to the gardens is a spectacular tableau of a broad walkway and zigzagging path that crosses a pond backed by palms, the wooded hillside of Montjuïc behind it. Huge buttresses of corten steel cut across the water. It is dramatic, beautiful and enticing.

A mauve and blue haze shimmers at the far end which, it turns out, belong to echiums and, in particular, *Echium candicans*, from Madeira. They were absolutely lovely – which I found rather disturbing. This is because until that moment, for over 60 years, I had truly believed that I disliked echiums. But a quick recalibration and acceptance of my faulty judgement and I was able to revel in their display, ranging from rich purple to the softest of blues set against the neighbouring yellow-green blaze from *Euphorbia lambii*, with unstinted admiration.

After an exceptionally dry winter, Barcelona had had a few days of rain the week before our visit

A billowing haze of pink flowers on the drought-loving grass *Muhlenbergia capillaris* softens the deliberately sharp-edged architecture of the garden.

A wide concrete path zigzags up the hillside, emphasising and creating the triangular motif repeated throughout the layout.

that spring and the hillside was alive with the prickle of flowers reaching out for their moment of glory in this briefest of Mediterranean springs.

The concrete path zigzags up the hillside following the overall design based upon triangles, the slopes buttressed by walls of rusted corten steel, with teucrium, gaura, nepeta and borage all flowering in a glaucous, delicate tangle. Higher up the slope, amongst the olives, deep plum-coloured poppies, like a wild 'Patty's Plum', phlomis and scabious were all covered with bees feeding voraciously. One area was a mass of pink valerian. A large white boulder was encased by cistus, the pink flowers floating at the end of its branches. A huge genista reached out across the path, flamboyantly smothered in bright yellow flowers. Lavender, santolina, rosemary and lemon verbena also flowered freely on the hillside, in home territory, adding a touch of familiar domesticity.

There is something hardcore and uncompromising about Mediterranean plants, especially in mid-Mediterranean summer, and they have evolved to withstand the conditions rather than thrive in them.

The city of Barcelona is glimpsed through the trunks of Washingtonia palms and the spent flower stems of huge echiums underplanted with cacti and agave.

The landscape designer Bet Figueras did much to improve the planting of the Barcelona Botanical Garden by creating a series of naturalised walks and vistas in which to display the plants at their best and to skilfully contextualise them.

Botanical gardens have to justify their existence by being interesting, educative and a valuable collection, but they do not always strive after aesthetic delight above botanical interest. However, the Barcelona Botanical Garden made a huge step in this direction when they commissioned Bet Figueras.

Bet was from Barcelona and had worked on the Olympic park and on projects such as the famous El Bulli restaurant. She set up her all-female practice in the city as well as teaching at the Barcelona School of Architecture. The landscaping was already completed when, in 1999, she was called in to make it less of a display of a plant collection and more of a garden. She did this by putting the plants into an environmental and ecological relationship, contextualising them. In contrast to the wide concrete roads zigzagging up the slopes, she made stone paths that wind across the hillside, just wide enough to walk in single file, while stepping over plants, round boulders and brushing beneath overhanging bushes.

The rather brutal architectural trope of triangles dominating the layout is humanised and softened. The dominant hand of man – and perhaps gender does play a role here – is tempered by the skilfully empathetic interplay of plants, stone and space. It is beautifully subtle because the plants are still on display, still all individually labelled and set in the correct groups and families, still accessible to academic study, but this does not override the easy beauty of their setting.

Bet's transformative work at the Botanical Garden won her a prestigious FAD (Fostering Architecture and Design) prize in 2000. However, she died at the height of her powers in 2010 at the age of 53. But not only does the Montjuïc hillside remain to be visited, enjoyed and to inspire, as the climate increasingly affects what and how we plant, her work is also becoming increasingly relevant to every garden in Mediterranean Spain.

Still gardening at 101, Joan Carulla has created a superbly productive plot filled with organic vegetables and fruit on the rooftop of his building high above the streets of Barcelona.

Joan Carulla
BARCELONA

WE FOUND OUR WAY TO AN UNREMARKABLE BARCELONA SIDE STREET WITH A HAIRDRESSER, white goods shop and old ladies having to pull their shopping trolleys into the street to round a double-parked lorry. The buzzer let me in and a lift took us up to the fifth floor. Joan Carulla greeted us at the door of his flat, leaning on a stick but dapper in jeans and warmly welcoming. His eyes were bright and there was an intensity, a focus, emanating from him. We sat down and made a kind of conversation – an unlikely exchange because his English is as non-existent as my Spanish, but it was one of those occasions when we sensed that we spoke the same language.

Joan was born in 1923 and brought up on a small farm near Lleida in the Catalan countryside. Franco especially hated the Catalans and life in Catalonia after the Civil War was appalling. The only thing that kept Joan and his family from starvation were the crops that they raised on their few acres of land. This need to grow to survive remained with him, despite moving to Barcelona and opening a supermarket, which he ran for many years. It was successful, he made some money, and 50 years ago he built this block of flats.

The fact that it had no garden did not deter him from gardening in a grand way. The large balcony was kitted out with tanks for collecting rainwater – 5,000 litres of it – with a drip-feed system to every container. In those containers today are tomatoes, a vine and decorative plants – a palm, ficus, monstera, sansevieria – all lustily healthy outside in Barcelona and all which would classify as houseplants in Britain, and so adding real exoticism to the rather anonymous building.

The tomatoes were more familiar territory for me. I have grown scores of varieties over the years, and yet could not place the ones Joan grows. It turns out that they are all 'Monserat'. He said that he grows these – has always and only ever grown them – because they are the best. Joan collects all his own seed from year to year. I learnt later that they are an old Catalan heritage variety, rarely available outside Catalonia. Growing and eating them is as much a statement of Catalan identity as a culinary preference.

Up a further couple of flights of stairs – the 101-year-old Joan leading the way – a small door opened to reveal an entire rooftop allotment. He said that they specially reinforced the building when it was constructed so that he could bring in 25 centimetres of soil – all carried up those flights of stairs in bags.

By the beginning of July the potatoes were already harvested – an early maincrop variety, 'Red Pontiac' – which, he said, need less water than most and have a white, waxy flesh. That is the farmer speaking: find a variety that works for you and stick with it. Don't try to be fancy. Go with the conditions and make the best of them.

A fig tree, almost entirely devoid of foliage, has gorgeously stripy fruit. A peach tree, set in a large oil can, has had all its fruit already harvested and eaten. Two nispero or loquat trees, with big leaves that look like they have been carefully folded and then unfolded to reveal the creases, are covered in unripe orange fruit. A large vine produces around 100 kilos of grapes each year, from which Joan makes wine, and there are recently lifted onions drying on the surface of the soil. A quarter of the roof space is occupied by garlic, small-headed and potent.

There are three or four compost bins of which Joan was rightly proud and everything that cannot be eaten goes back into the soil via them. It is clearly a well-worked, well-used, well-loved plot that happens to be on top of a building in a Barcelonian side street. But by early July it was noticeably bare. It is too hot and dry for most vegetables. The water Joan collects in tanks on the roof lasts for 11 months of the year. But Joan said it is getting hotter and drier every year. In the past two years, he has lost 18 fruit trees, including figs, nispero, citrus and plum. All the earthworms have gone, he said, which he puts down to the birds eating them. I suggested that it is because it is getting warmer and they cannot get deep enough in the shallow soil of the roof to keep cool. He smiled and gave me a forgiving look. Through our eyes alone we agreed to amicably differ.

Joan used to grow sweetcorn, beans and a wider variety of vegetables, and, until he was 95, did all the digging and cultivation himself. But he had an accident and that slowed him down – although not enough to stop him climbing four flights of stairs to do all the work needed to raise potatoes, grapes, onions and garlic here and his 'Monserat' tomatoes on the balcony below.

Joan does all his planting in March, in the last quarter of the old moon. This is traditional Catalan lore rather than New Agery. He is organic through long habit and necessity rather than ideology. He has the practical sufficiency of the true countryman, despite all these years living here in

Barcelona. The garden is not beautiful. Everything is recycled, upcyled, rejigged and adapted. Baler twine, random pieces of wood, scaffolding, plastic poles, bits of nylon netting and every kind of plastic container are put to use. You can take the boy out of the farm but, for all the city streets and high-rise buildings crowding in on all sides, you cannot take the farm out of the very old man.

I asked Joan the secret of living so evidently well to 101. Well, he said, he never smoked, does not drink, did not touch meat for most of his life and – he added with weighted significance – never learnt to drive so rode a bike everywhere. But above all, he tried to follow the rule of eights, he explained: eight hours work, eight hours engagement helping others and eight hours sleep.

As I leave we embrace and it feels like a blessing. 'Come back next spring,' he said. 'Come back when everything is still growing.' Perhaps that is the secret of a long and good life that every gardener understands – next spring, when everything is growing.

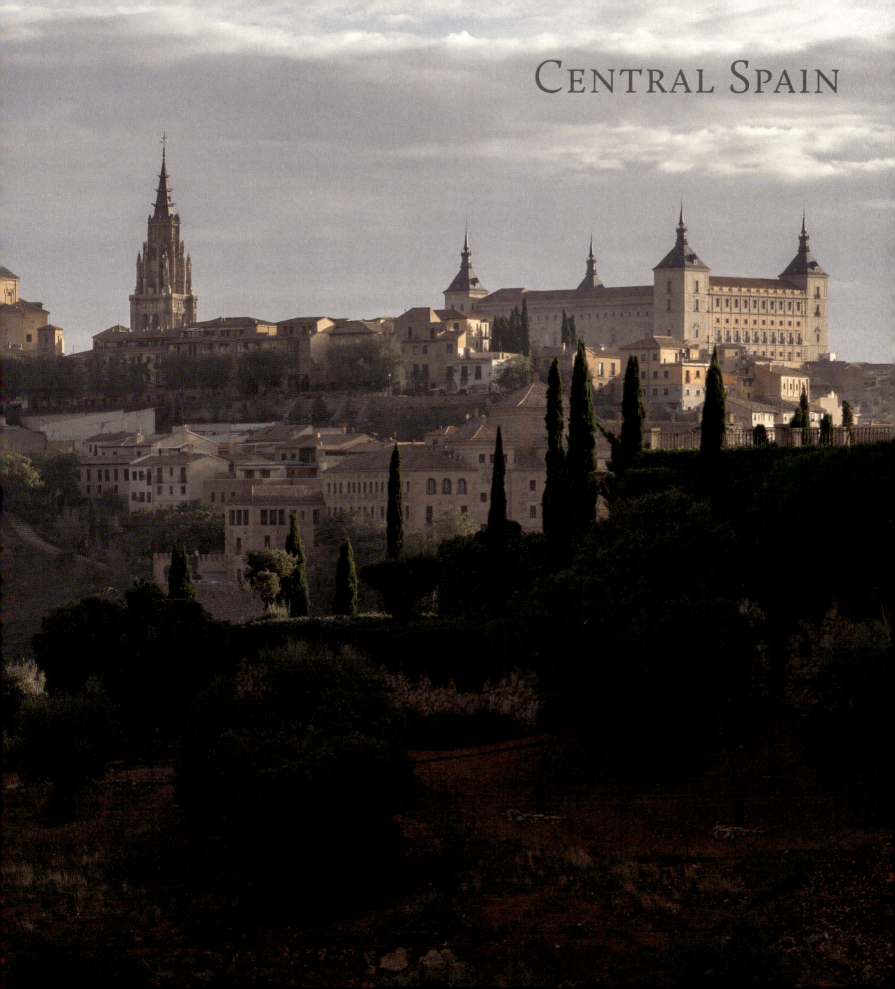

CENTRAL SPAIN

Previous spread: A view across the gorge of the Tagus River to the old town of Toledo with the fortress of the Alcázar and cathedral spire rising above the pink stones of surrounding buildings.

Opposite: The one-acre tropical garden planted in the 1990s on redundant tracks and platforms of Madrid's central Atocha station is now soaringly mature.

Atocha Station
MADRID

You arrive from Seville by the super-efficient high-speed train, having had the best view of and, as ever, marvelling at the vastness and emptiness of the Spanish hinterland. You grab your bags, join the crowd flowing to the exit and a search for a cab. But the rain is biblical and you don't have an umbrella and are standing in a long queue getting soaked. So, just like I did, you decide to have a coffee and wait until the rain eases. This also gives an opportunity to enjoy one of the least likely and best gardens in any railway station in the world.

The original Atocha building at the end of the Paseo del Prado is a wrought iron, handsome remnant of the 1892 station that became defunct in the 1990s when the new high-speed train linking Seville and Madrid came into operation. This left a large, vaulted space of about an acre, with three unused lines and their platforms. But instead of pulling it down it was decided to fill that space with a tropical garden. The result is a glorious hybrid of enormous glasshouse and railway station disappearing gracefully into jungle, the plants forming three thick borders where the tracks were and the platforms made into paths flanked with seats beneath the green shade.

I first saw it in the summer of 2006 but was in a hurry to change trains and had no time to linger. But nearly two decades later, with the rain showing no sign of letting up, it became the ideal place to sit and let travel and weather and bustle all rearrange themselves into a manageable shape. The really extraordinary and wonderful thing about the planting in Atocha station is that it is so generous and untrammelled. The whole thing is on a scale proportionate to the building but bigger and more extreme than anything that most of us ever come across in our daily lives – and especially so here in the middle of sun-blasted, ice-scoured Spain.

There is a generosity of vision as well as planting. There are over 200 species with more than 7,000 plants, many from the once global Spanish Empire, with rubber trees from South America, cacao from Central America, royal palms and mahogany from Cuba, and bananas from the Philippines. A misting system kicks in when the temperature reaches 35 degrees, keeping the plants healthy and happy.

Travellers seem happy too. People sit reading or talking, a surprising number with small dogs and some stretched out on the raised stone edging to the beds, earbuds in. All the incessant movement or its imminence that builds anxiety into the fabric of every train station and airport had stopped for precious, deeply civilised moments, courtesy of the plants. Their scale and green heft dictates the pace and atmosphere in a powerful and effective way. I am sure the reason for creating the planting was to look dramatic, but in fact, the real effect is that it makes everyone feel relaxed.

Why have not more stations and airports learnt from this? The only disappointment is that the two ponds inside the planting (inaccessible to visitors) are now livestock free. They once housed refugee turtles, rescued from the sewers and drains of the city after they had been abandoned by bored owners and rehomed here, but a few years ago were moved to a more suitable site. Pity – a turtle or two would have made the wonderful perfect.

There are over 7,000 plants from more than 200 species in the garden, mostly tropical and dramatically lush like the enormous leaves of this elephant's ear alocasia.

Crisply cut box parterres run down the centre of the Paseo de las Estatuas that runs from the Puerta de España down the middle of the Retiro, flanked by statues of Spanish worthies – and on a perfect April evening, the chestnuts are all in full flower.

The Retiro
MADRID

My hotel window obligingly faced across Calle de Alfonso XII to the Retiro park and the canopy of mature trees spreading out from there. From above, they looked unbroken, but at ground level the trees are intersected by hundreds of paths mostly hedged, like an Italian *bosco*. It is woodland, but ornate and carefully tended, made for walking and picnicking.

Go up the steps and through the gates and you are facing a long promenade with parterres of low, wide box running down the middle, flanked by statues of Spanish worthies through the ages. Western twenty-first-century park life barely varies from country to country. The hierarchy of jogging is the same, with the serious runners weaving dismissively through the more sedate but often beautifully kitted out plodders, dogs half dragging many of them along. In fact, there were lots of dogs of all kinds, surprisingly well-behaved and regularly meeting fellow canine companions in what is obviously a daily social occasion. But all great parks have their own atmosphere and character, and, in this, the Retiro is idiosyncratic and distinctly of Madrid.

This is no accident. Until 1868, the Retiro was a royal park attached to the Buen Retiro Palace, built in the 1630s for Philip IV. The name describes its role as a secondary royal palace, designated for recreation. It remains true to that purpose, albeit shorn of both palace and royal connection. The Buen Retiro housed the huge equestrian portraits of Philip III and his wife, Margaret of Austria, as well as Philip IV, Isabella of Bourbon and the young and doomed Prince Balthasar Carlos, all ready to gallop through the park in pursuit of deer and pleasure – albeit with a stretch of the imagination as the first two died before the Retiro was built and Prince Carlos and his mother barely lasted much longer. No matter. It set the tone.

As well as a royal hunting ground, like the Boboli Gardens in Florence, the Retiro was used for elaborate mock battles, bullfights and theatrical displays. It was a place of play and a deliberate retreat from the business of government associated with the Palacio Real. But when Napoleon's troops were barracked there after their arrival in Madrid in 1808, they trashed the buildings, cut down or blew up most of the trees – it is said that a solitary tree survives from pre-Napoleonic occupation – and dug up the gardens.

When the city took ownership in 1868, the park was completely replanted and remodelled, and the public allowed unlimited access – making it the first park in the world to be open to every citizen. Now, 150 years on, the mid-nineteenth-century replanting has reached an almost ideal maturity, with many trees fully grown but not yet succumbing to the frailties of age. There are over 15,000 in the 125 hectares and they cast a delicious dappled green shade. Because of their proximity to each other, they grow tall and slender, reaching for the light, reinforcing the sense of a carefully orchestrated woodland. I have been in winter, summer, autumn and, on the last but most perfect occasion, in April, when all the horse chestnuts – and there are a lot of them in the Retiro – were in exuberant, dancing flower.

Other than the human pleasure that reverberates through the trees, avenues and open spaces, the main feature of the Retiro is its hedges. They are everywhere, containing and delineating paths, enclosing areas amongst the trees into hundreds of little fields or *boscos*. As the gentle slopes rise or fall, the horizontal lines of their clipped tops create layer upon layer of sloping, stretching, tightly clipped green, falling diagonally and in dead straight planes, cut and intersected by tree trunks.

In some areas, the grass, despite the shade, is surprisingly green and tightly mown, so perfect for picnics, and in others, the understory has been allowed to grow more freely, providing cover for wildlife. The flowers of philadelphus, viburnum and elder make the paths heady with their scent.

There is the great Palacio de Cristal, with its Basque iron structure holding together glass walls and roof, modelled apparently on London's Crystal Palace and built to house an exhibition on the Philippines in the 1880s, but which is now a completely empty, light-filled space used for art exhibitions. There is the rectangular lake, the Estanque del Retiro, one of the few remaining features of the original palace gardens and formerly the site for mock naval battles and watery theatricals, now filled with small boats veering like dodgems, rowed by young men with sleeves rolled to show their rippling arm muscles to their admiring passengers.

There are rose gardens, formal gardens, the man-made Montaña de los Gatos, or 'Cat Mountain', tight in one corner, fountains aplenty, a theatre and a range of diversions and entertainments that honour the original spirit of the royal palace – which was somewhere to escape the burden of responsible life and be entertained.

But for all its many and varied entertainments on offer, the hundreds of walks between the hedges, through and under the superb trees of the park, especially on a glorious spring evening with the sunlight caught in the fresh foliage of the trees, are reason and entertainment enough. It exists to be enjoyed and no park I have ever visited fulfils that purpose better.

The Retiro has many discreet but safe wooded areas with paths lined by hedges, creating sheltered spots in the middle of the city where people read, picnic, exercise or just sit quietly enjoying the rich canopy of green.

Below: At the weekend the park is full of performance artists, buskers and entertainers – here a clown captivates a group of passing children with magic tricks.

Opposite: The Palacio de Cristal, built in the 1880s and modelled on London's Crystal Palace, is a huge light-filled space used for art exhibitions.

Santander Bank

MADRID

THERE IS OFTEN A BLAND HORTICULTURAL UNIFORMITY THAT SPREADS FROM CORPORATE headquarters to hotel to service station with all the individuality and charisma of factory-produced paintings inside the rooms of chain hotels. It is designed to decorate and hide in a trouble-free and aseasonal way, but not distract or divert you. It is horticultural muzak. But sometimes, the mould is broken. Sometimes, credit has to be given to a corporation – in this case a bank – for doing something truly inspiring.

A short walk north of the Prado is the Banco Pastor Building in Paseo de Recoletos. It is an unremarkable office block, built in the 1970s and now owned by Santander bank, with automatic glass doors and a café looking out onto the street occupied by figures hunched over laptops. So far so unremarkable or even interesting. But what makes it extraordinary is that as part of the building's construction, the bank commissioned a young, practically unknown designer to create a garden in the awkward space between this and the neighbouring office. His name was Luis González-Camino and he is now renowned as one of Spain's leading landscape architects – but back in 1975, when he got the job, he was barely 21 and almost no one had heard of him.

Luis met me at the bank, as much, I am sure, to review the garden as to see me, but he spoke flawless English and was generous with his time and memories of the project.

'I remember realising that in all the meetings – and there were a lot of meetings – that I was always the youngest in the room,' he said.

It is to the credit of the very middle-aged bankers that not only did they choose Luis for the job in the first place but that they encouraged the young designer to have his head.

His plan was simple enough: 'I wanted to make a lush, green space that the people working in the building could both enjoy and benefit from.'

But back in the mid-seventies, the concept of plants being 'good' for you was never expressed, if ever thought. Gardens of any kind were to be looked at and admired or appreciated. Any benefits were aesthetic rather than the very modern idea of 'well-being'. But, even if not articulated, Luis instinctively knew that plants could do this. He was – and very much still is – a gardener too. He had been in charge of his family garden in Cantabria, just south of Santander, since he was 18. It is the lodestone that he constantly returns to and which gives him an unusually hands-on understanding of how plants grow as well as how they might look to their best advantage.

The site in the bank was hardly easy. The two buildings are separated by a long, thin gap, about three metres wide and rising up over twenty metres on all four sides. The ground is gravelled and has palms fountaining out from tall planters. Look up, as the space narrows to accommodate the overhanging planting terraces, and high up you see light coming through a glass roof, creating a very tall, almost chimney-like greenhouse.

On the bank side there are glass windows opening to offices on each floor, and on the other, a sheer wall eight storeys high. Luis planted English ivy in planters along the top of this wall and it quickly cascaded down – some strands of the original plants have grown the full 24 metres (although the garden was revamped and plants renewed and replaced in 2020). The effect of this very simple device of an enormous green curtain is both beautiful and immediately calming. The bankers, toiling over their numbers, look out onto the shimmering emerald interplay of the leaves, lit at a slant from the angled skylight, and doubtless feel a little better about their office-bound lives.

But that is not all. Two floors of the bank building have metre-wide planting terraces filled with a rich mixture of tropical plants, so that the workers look through these to the wall of ivy, and the light coming into the rooms has to slide past and through this lushly exotic planting.

The effect is similar to the way that so many younger people sharing houses or living in flats with no outdoor space now use houseplants. It humanises and enriches an otherwise sterile and bland space. But this was created 50 years ago when houseplants were definitely uncool and rarely found in offices – and certainly not on this scale. It was, in its own green way, revolutionary and perhaps significant that it was done in 1975, the year of Franco's death, the year when Spain burst free from its past and when youth and creativity was – at last – unleashed.

The garden ingeniously fills a narrow, awkward space between two buildings and yet creates a real sense of rich growth as well as an intimate, green space to sit in.

Opposite: One of the owner's chocolate Labradors takes a morning stroll in his garden amongst the billows of stachys and glowing flower heads of *Euphorbia characias*.

Overleaf: The dog garden, with its loose arrangement of gravel paths and plants, is set below the rigid horizontal lines of the house and its immediate formal planting.

Álvaro Sampedro Dog Garden
MADRID

AS SOMEONE WHOSE LIFE HAS BEEN MEASURED OUT IN THE DOGS THAT I HAVE LOVED, THE DRAW of a self-styled 'dog garden' was always going to be irresistible. The fact that it had been designed by the landscape designer Álvaro Sampedro was both enticing and slightly disappointing as I had rather liked the image of hounds at the drawing board and carefully placing plants. As it happens, the garden is a combination of both human and canine design and lives up to all expectations.

The house is in a wealthy suburb of tree-lined roads bounded by large houses behind high walls and electronic gates, their ubiquitous swimming pools sensed if not seen. No doubt most have gyms. A golf course, of course, laps about the end of the road.

Álvaro Sampedro was commissioned to create a garden around the gleaming white new build that would be ideal 'for dogs'. Resisting the temptation to fence it off and bury a series of bones, balls and perhaps introduce a colony of rabbits and a squirrel or two – which would certainly be my dog's idea of horticultural heaven – Álvaro took the project seriously. He was there at the garden to show me around and explain that when he made his first visit with his own dogs, he watched how they moved around the space, following scent trails, repeatedly following the same routes in response to knocks at the gate or the barking of neighbouring dogs. A pattern of sorts emerged and he based his design upon these doggy tracks.

Álvaro is a superb and much-respected designer, as well as a dog lover, so this was no quirky, off-the-wall project. The garden is lovely, be you human, dog or any other sentient creature. It flows. The planting reflects not just the whims of the dogs but the inescapable conditions of all central Spanish gardens – poor soil and a frighteningly harsh climate that is fiercely hot and dry in summer and equally challenging in winter, with temperatures often falling into double figures below zero.

Clipped cushions of phillyrea and escallonia buffer the house from the pillow with the dog garden down steps on the lower level.

The initial clay was improved with the addition of a freer-draining loam and the planting is limited to that which will cope with the climate without any protection other than an irrigation system.

Outside the low-slung white house with its huge plate glass windows, blinds firmly down to screen sun and prying eyes, is the inevitable pool with its adjacent outdoor kitchen, a parterre made from entwined billows of phillyrea and escallonia clipped into flowing abstract shapes, softening the rigidity of the building. So far, entirely predictable in a perfectly handsome but unengaged way. But the good bit, the doggy bit, is beyond on a lower level.

It is not a big space but it is subdivided effectively into different areas entire unto themselves by a drop in level and a change in planting and tone. Steps lead down past terraces of the grasses miscanthus 'Gracillimus' and panicum 'Heavy Metal'. A low myrtle hedge divides the line of grasses falling to the level below.

This is where the dog action really comes into play. The planting is simple, informal and, early on the spring morning that I visited, elegantly beautiful. *Euphorbia characias* positively glowed and a side path running the whole length of the garden was completely lined with it, making the most dramatic display of its inner yallery-green luminescence I have ever seen. White valerian, *Verbena bonariensis*, stachys, tansy and *Euphorbia characias* repeated themselves at random, clearly self-sown, but with a harmonious rhythm.

In the centre of this area is seating made from polished concrete built around a fire pit. It is bunkerlike and a little brutal against the softness of the planting but, Álvaro told me, designed to withstand the extremes of the climate. Against one corner of this seating area is the lone tree in this space (the whole exterior is shielded by pines, screening golf course and neighbours), an *Acer x freemanii*.

Gravel paths wind through the planting, themselves patterned with young, self-sown seedlings, all left to establish themselves as and how they may. These are the dog paths, twisting through the space. Álvaro told me that they were not fixed and changed slightly from season to season, but that the planting could adapt and accommodate this. They lifted and replanted some things, allowed others to be trampled and relied on self-seeding to fill other gaps.

It is a fascinating idea of a garden that is untethered, constantly on the move. I came across a similar concept in the garden of Gilles Clément, La Vallée, in Creuse, central France. The essence of this approach is that there is no 'right' place for a plant other than where it chooses to grow. Much of conventional gardening resists this, but to do so is, in the long run at least, a losing battle. All plants will eventually find where they most want to be in any given situation and, as I know only too well from my own garden – some plants, that might be very happy with a neighbour, just do not want to grow in my backyard.

Álvaro deals with this with a quiet, competent practicality. 'Don't fight with nature,' he says. 'You will lose.' So he relies upon a smallish group of what he calls 'superplants' that will survive and adapt in the given situation. They tend to be native species and many could be found growing well in the immediate area around the garden. It follows that every different combination of soil, climate and situation will need a different set of superplants, but having established what these are – like the valerian, euphorbia, salvia, phillyrea, myrtle, ceonothus and stipas in this garden – use them to form the bulk of the planting and then let them go where they will.

It is not 'rewilding' in any way because the whole thing is carefully curated. It is monitored, selected and gardened. There are undesirable weeds that are removed. The shrubs are tightly and skilfully clipped. Making new paths involves removing plants where the dogs have chosen to go. But it is a looser relationship than many gardeners use or might feel comfortable with.

The two hefty chocolate house Labradors, Pod and Pepa, both broad across the beam and used to an unhurried life, plod and sway through the planting, rarely rising to more than a trot, whereas Álvaro's own goldendoodle Juana (a charming cross between poodle and golden retriever) has a soft-limbed obsession with a tennis ball that has her crashing and dashing through the planting in a way that would be a disaster in most borders but which here is happily indulged.

The result is a very modern way of planting, adapted to climate change and low maintenance, yet stylish and looking very good – with the added wit and charm of being distinctly doggy. But it is exceptional. Many Spaniards, especially the wealthy ones that can afford to live in places like this, still think that a garden must have a lawn. Most do not really engage with the daily intricacies of gardening, wanting a garden to perform and be there in the same way that the pool or the fire pit is. In other words, these horticultural developments are not driven by the demands of clients, but by the ingenuity and skill of designers like Álvaro and his contemporaries, who are not making gardens in spite of the prevailing conditions, but embracing them to create something sustainable and inspiring.

Every aspect of the Colegio Reggio is designed to be ecologically and environmentally interrelated. The exterior with its porthole windows is clad in cork that as well as providing insulation is intended as a growing environment for fungi, plants and insects.

Colegio Reggio
MADRID

LA MORELEJA IS RINGED ENTIRELY BY MOTORWAYS. DIAGONALLY ACROSS THIS LOOSE CIRCLE FROM the dog garden, over the wealth boundary and into Encinar de los Reyes, an area of smaller, more tightly packed houses, is a new school that has incorporated plants and gardens as part of the fabric of the structure, completely integrating the process and results of growing and living with plants.

I happened to hear about it on a brief winter trip to Madrid and we stopped off on our way back to the airport to have a recce. The school building, designed by Andrés Jaque, sits in a patch of wasteland with its zigzag roof sprouting chimneys like aluminium periscopes and porthole windows set in cork cladding – designed not just to insulate, which it apparently is very good at, but also to deliberately provide an environment for lichens, mosses, plants and a range of potential small creatures.

The architecture of the school is based on the idea that buildings are never just for people but are part of the habitat around them in all its forms and manifestations. It is also as unconcealed as possible in every aspect, so that the exposed details of the architecture will stimulate a desire for exploration and explanation. Thus, the building is deliberately composed of a number of educational 'ecosystems'. All the ingredients, the thousand component parts that make up any building, from mortar to wiring to heating ducts to polished floor, are exposed and open to scrutiny. The whole building is intended as an integral, coherent educational interaction, a library of practical materials and resources to be used as part of the student's education.

The gardens work in the same way. From the very beginning, the architects included a linked series of green spaces, at ground level and on each storey – often blurring the boundary between inside and outside – that consisted of individual little gardens, making one larger horticultural element that was integral to the building and the experience of the school's pupils.

So the children can see the plants grow, see how they change across the seasons, see how butterflies and pollinating insects and perhaps even nesting birds all come and visit, and which plants they choose. As well as being fun, it is profoundly good education. The gardens enter into every possible conjunction and cross-fertilisation of all the subjects that the pupils might be engaged in, in the same way that the heating system or the construction of the round porthole windows are too.

I visited the school again in spring. The gardens had come alive, adding a lushness to the graphic outlines of the building. Outside, a class of five-year-olds were harvesting their lunch from raised beds where they had grown very healthy-looking cabbages, leaf celery, chard and leeks. They chattered and fidgeted and squabbled but were clearly having fun. And, for the record, the vegetables all looked really good by any gardening standards. When the harvest was gathered, the children then planted tomatoes and peppers into the beds with the aplomb and confidence of seasoned allotment holders.

Eva Martín, the principal, has driven the project from its conception. She exudes a calm, smiling dynamism that clearly inspires staff and children alike. There was an atmosphere of collusion that I had not experienced at any of my own or my children's schools – that is to say, a sense of mutual purpose and intent of everyone involved, from the five-year-olds to the teenagers kicking a ball around in the bare yard – to make the experience as good and life-enhancing as possible. As Eva described it to me, 'The invisibles are made visible.' The gardens are an integral part of that revelation.

The biggest garden is indoors, in the atrium, where seats are set in gravel amongst lush green palms, rubber plants and tall ficus trees that rise towards the curved glass roof three storeys above. The walls are painted green with green tendrils of ivy making their way up them, green doubling down on green. This makes an ad hoc classroom as well as a place for pupils to meet and relax, the two usually mutually exclusive activities seemingly happily coexisting within the informality of the space and its planting.

Up on the second and third floors, large plate glass windows give out onto generous flat areas between gable ends, planted intensively with trees, shrubs and annuals. They operate as a cross between roof gardens and gigantic window boxes. These busy borders and their attendant wildlife – the flowers were frantic with bees collecting nectar when I visited in spring – high up on the side of the building are designed to be studied closely from the inside, rather like the glass viewing wall of an aquarium, and assimilated into the general form and outline of the building from the outside.

Gardens in or attached to schools tend to be a token, intended as an introduction to the idea of plants and wildlife and our interaction with them. This is obviously to be applauded, but it comes wrapped about with fairly low aspirations, aiming to be good enough rather than to create something special in its own right. But the planting and various aspects of the gardens at Colegio Reggio have no such inhibitions. They ooze confidence and aspiration, openly intending to be as beautiful and stimulating as might possibly be – not least to provide the best education for the children.

The principal, Eva Martín, has driven the project from conception to curriculum.

Opposite: An atrium on the ground floor is used as an alternative classroom and meeting space and filled with lush green palms, rubber plants and tall ficus trees that rise towards the curved glass roof, three storeys above.

Below: Every classroom has large windows reaching to ground level so the exterior is constantly part of the pupil's scenery.

A view from the patio across the formal pool, festooned with plants, to the landscape of the estate beyond with its oaks growing in the wheat fields and the wooded hillside behind.

Los Molinillos
MADRID

Los Molinillos, a 40-minute drive west out of Madrid, is a hunting estate belonging to the Urquijo family. The land stretches out to the horizon, encompassing vast fields of wheat growing amongst holm oaks. The stables, half a mile from the house, include tack rooms filled with ranks of beautifully worked high-backed saddles, and around the main house is an immaculately maintained garden that is lodged firmly in the Spain of the 1960s and 1970s. As such, it is a fascinating insight into a world that has been very significant and influential throughout Spain's modern history. And as well as providing a glimpse into Spain's past, it is also a very hospitable, much loved family home.

The matriarch of the estate is Piru Urquijo, who, at 88, is still very fit, with a mind that is razor sharp. She speaks perfect English, rich with the idioms of her youth. Charming, attentive, not suffering fools at all, she knows everyone, remembers everything and misses nothing.

Piru first came here in 1957 when her husband, Jaime, inherited the house. 'It was,' she told me, 'one of Spain's best shooting estates.' Given the Spanish patrician class's almost obsessive love of hunting in all its forms, that made it very special indeed. I suspect it still is.

Although the estate is old and the family even older, the house was rebuilt in 1944 by an American architect. He created a building in the traditional Spanish style but with all the modern conveniences of contemporary America. Piru said that the local workmen assumed that in fact they were building an exclusive hotel because the design included a bathroom for each and every bedroom – unheard of in Spain at that time.

Whilst the American aspect of the building may include the luxuries of unlimited hot water, the Spanish element includes a large patio that the house wraps around, creating a central courtyard bedecked with flowers, with views across a long rectangular basin, framed within clipped box and

cypress hedging, out to the fields and hills beyond. Always, in this central part of the country, you are reminded of the ferocity of the summer heat and the absolute need for shade and coolness. This creates an interaction between house and garden, and, at Los Molinillos, the landscape beyond, with the house bleeding into the patio which in turn drifts into the garden almost without division.

When Piru arrived as a young bride at the end of the 1950s, the garden was 'very French and very pretty'. By this, I took her to mean more floral and more formal. However, the arrival of children changed all that.

'We had an English nanny who said there was no place for the children to play and for her to promenade the pram. So we pulled the old garden up and then we had much more fun here on the lawn.'

We were talking at the edge of a large lawn to one side of the house, bright green at the end of one of the driest summers recorded, thanks to the sprinklers that rise automatically from their subterranean bunkers. She told me that these are used all the year round to keep the grass a suitably

Los Molinillos has a number of areas of carefully tended, lush green grass, originally created for children to play on but increasingly hard to maintain as the climate changes.

The entrance gates lead to the house which, although completely rebuilt in the 1940s, is the heart of one of Spain's oldest and grandest sporting estates.

English green and the French formality was sacrificed to the games of Piru's six children.

The garden has now evolved from those nanny-inspired changes into something comfortable, solid and impressive, rather like well-used but very expensive furniture that has been part of a large household for generations. The cypress and box hedges have become baggy and slightly loose with age but are tightly clipped, and so, instead of being dishevelled, have acquired the careless charm of the roué gone slightly to seed but still wearing exquisitely tailored clothes. They lean and bend in either side of the long path by the side of the house, buttressing the plants around the lawn and edging the rose beds in the rose garden with what amounts to a spreading midriff. A magnificent stone pine sculpts the sky around it, catching the evening's sun whilst the ground below falls into deep shadow. Beyond it, the hundreds of green holm oaks stand in ground parched tawny brown despite recent rains.

But for all its charm and care, Los Molinillos is not really sustainable as a twenty-first-century garden, with the demands and impact of the changing climate, nor is it an historic remnant to be carefully preserved. It is, in many ways, caught between changing worlds.

As well as a long drought that spring and summer, there had been terrible flooding just a few weeks before my visit to Los Molinillos, worse than anything Piru had experienced there. The garden, on a slope up above most of the surrounding land, was unaffected, but horses had to be rescued to avoid drowning, and it had obviously been deeply shocking.

As in the rest of the world, Spanish gardeners are having to adapt and change the plants they use and how they grow them and, consequentially, the style of gardens. Piru shook her head at these new water-wise, climate-adapted gardens. 'They look like Arizona,' she said, not meaning it as a compliment.

However, the landscape and the climate around Los Molinillos is not so different from Arizona. Despite the recent flooding, the ground is parched and bare, and a few saguaro cacti would not look out of place. The future of this kind of richly green garden, inspired by the English gardens of the 1950s and 1960s, looks bleak. I asked Piru what she thought her garden would be like in 50 years' time. 'I hate to think,' she said. 'Everything is going to change tremendously and drastically.'

Piru is right, of course. The Spanish relationship between house and patio, and a life lived as much outdoors as in, will remain and adapt. But the lush lawns and rose gardens and green walls of the hedges that have provided the backdrop to a large growing family, grand shooting parties, weddings and countless house guests over the past 60 years, and the complicated mixture of influences from across Europe, is all unsustainable in the modern world. Everything, as Piru says, is going to change tremendously.

Left: Los Molinillos has its own chapel with the bell tolling the services.

Opposite: Much of the household's communal life is led outside on the patios that ring the house, sheltered from the force of the sun.

Reflected in the water of the pond, the granite walls of the monastic buildings of El Escorial were intended to intimidate and impress with its scale and austerity.

El Escorial
MADRID

SAN LORENZO DE EL ESCORIAL IS A GRANITE ROCK FACE THAT IS A FORBIDDING SYMBOL OF ecclesiastic and regal power and authority. Its scale is monumental and there is something of an asylum about its sheer walls with their small, even, cell-like windows. It is a monastery, palace and garden, and combines all these things with imposition and contradiction. You cannot help but be intimidated, subdued and a little confused.

All of this is deliberate, or at least consistent with its place in Spanish history. When Philip II took over the kingdom of Spain from his father, Charles V, in 1556, he was in Flanders and did not return to Spain until three years later. During that time, he had been king of England through his marriage to Mary Tudor. But the Spain he returned to, despite its vast empire stretching from the Americas to the Netherlands, and most of Italy, had no physical or governmental centre. The court trooped from city to city in a vast train of pack animals and courtiers. There was no capital and no central focal point to the country, which was still a loosely conjoined group of provinces dominated by Castile that barely held together. So, in 1561, Philip settled on Madrid as his capital, not least because it was in the centre of the country, and had good water and parks where he could indulge his passion for hunting.

Philip wanted to create a monastery within striking distance of Madrid that would also serve as a palace, library and mausoleum. In 1563, work began to build the monastery for the order of Hieronymite monks in El Escorial, at the foot of the Guadarrama mountains, the site having been chosen for its supply of local granite and because it was just 50 kilometres – a day's journey – northwest of Madrid. The initial design was made by Juan Bautista de Toledo and continued after his death to its completion in 1584 by Juan de Herrera.

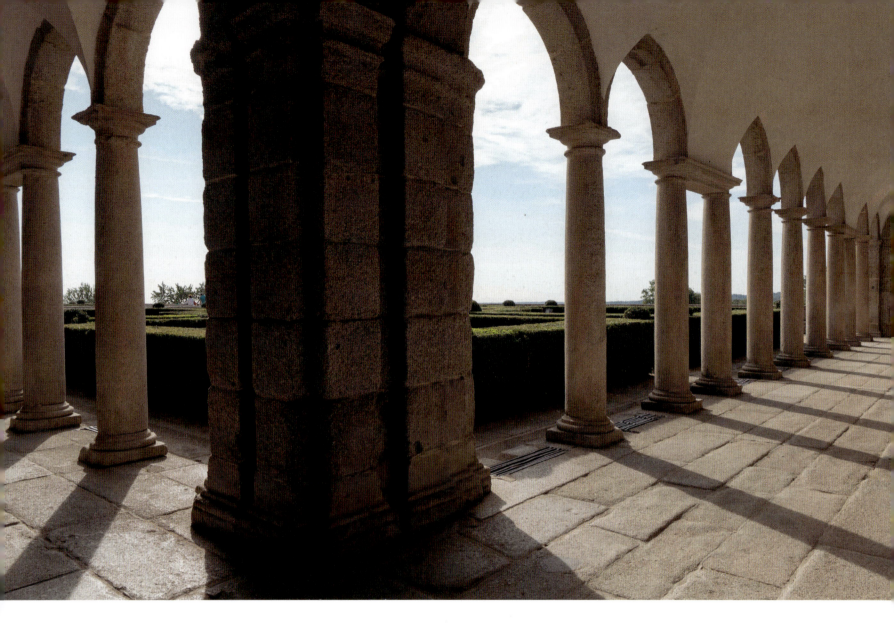

Everything about the building is in excess. There are over 2,600 windows, 1,200 doors, 86 staircases, 89 fountains and over 150 kilometres of corridors. The library has over 40,000 volumes, constituting one of Europe's great Renaissance libraries. A mausoleum down in the bowels of the building, decked in gleaming gold and ebony, and managing to be both gloomy and kitsch, houses the mummified bodies of most of the Spanish royal family from Charles V to Alfonso XIII. The bodies were first placed in the *pudridero*, the rotting room, before, having sufficiently composted down, placed in sarcophagi and slid into niches around the octagonal chamber.

All this was overseen by Philip himself. El Escorial is first and foremost his building, his monument and, as with everything in his strange, obsessive life, he micro managed every detail.

Philip loved the outdoors, which, as for any monarch or aristocrat of the period, centred around hunting, but he also loved gardens, especially as a result of his time in Flanders in the 1550s, and brought back with him ideas, designs and plants that were new to Spain. Added to this was the influx

The box hedges of the parterres on the western terrace butt tight to the cloisters of the monks' infirmary and hospice.

The large rectangular pond, buttressed by huge granite walls and walkways, was built primarily to hold fish for the many meat-free days in the Catholic calendar.

of plants from the Americas and the influence of Italian Renaissance gardens that were being made in this period via Philip's rule of the Habsburg southern half of Italy.

He sent his royal gardeners to Northern Europe to visit gardens and gather inspiration and knowledge, commissioned paintings of orchards and gardens as reference, and personally ordered myrtles and acacias from Valencia. In the royal palace at Aranjuez (that I went to visit only to find it closed and inaccessible due to storm damage), he commissioned nearly quarter of a million trees and supervised the planting of all of them.

The gardens at El Escorial start as a wide set of parterres around two sides of the palace (with the other two sides paved with huge granite slabs to create an effect as intimidating and dominating as the building itself), then, accessed by giant granite-covered stairways, the next level down was orchards of almonds, olives, oranges and pomegranates, and beyond that he planted thousands of trees. All of this was encircled by a wall and amounted to some 50 square kilometres of planted, managed land.

Opposite: Phillip II ordered roses to be planted along the base of the western walls so that the unadorned sheer granite would seem to float in a cloud of flowers. Today this is replicated by the modern climbing rose 'Mary Delaney', selected for its robustness in coping with the extremes of heat and cold experienced by central Spain.

Right: Columns framing the distant hills that Philip acquired so he could indulge his passion for hunting.

Around the base of the building is a curtain of climbing roses – or rather, one particular rose, a modern English variety called 'Mary Delaney', selected for its similarity to images of the original chosen (of course) by Philip himself and its robustness in coping with the extremes of heat and cold experienced by central Spain. It is also said that Philip wanted them to give the effect of the granite walls seeming to float on a cloud of rose petals.

In Philip's day, the parterres would have been filled with a combination of flowers, including some that were beginning to come in from the new American colonies, and coloured stones to create knot gardens laid out like carpets or tapestries to be viewed from above, rather than parterres which emanated from France a century later and tended to consist solely of the ornate patterns created by the hedging without any infill. But the idea was the same and much of the planting of the box parterres there now dates back to the Bourbon period of the mid-eighteenth century.

One of the most notable things about the formal gardens around the building is how flat the planes are. Just as the vertical plane of the building is almost uninterrupted and without embellishment, so too the horizontal plane of the garden is also uninterrupted. The result is that there are no volumes, no sense of spaces created by objects. Nothing of what the Japanese would call *ma*. The platform of the garden around the building acts almost like a moat, protecting and encircling it rather than being an inviting domestic space. It is all of a piece with the austerity and insularity of the entire place.

Within the monastery, the Cloister of the Evangelists is one of the largest courtyard gardens in the world. It is dominated – to an overpowering degree – by a vast domed pavilion with sculptures of the evangelists and four large stone basins. This was the monk's physic garden, although it is now laid out with four ornate box-hedged parterres. For all its impressiveness, it has an institutionalised lack of personal love or involvement, like the garden of an expensive hotel. But perhaps there is only so much magnificence humankind can bear in one day.

The best place to see the garden is from the king's chambers on the north corner of the palace. The rooms are surprisingly modest for the richest and most powerful sovereign in the world. A small window opens out onto the king's garden, walled off from the rest of the northern parterre and where he would walk. As he lay dying in the small bed, Philip had one window looking in on the basilica so he could hear mass being said and the other out onto his garden, with a view out to the landscape beyond until it fades to a smudge against the sky.

Within all the vastness of this forbidding granite building, it seems that this scene encapsulates the elements of Philip and Spain of the sixteenth century – which is perhaps an important aspect of Spain still. The church at its heart coupled with the power and control of a central ruler, the garden outside stocked with plants from all over the world, along with a stream of seemingly limitless wealth, and then the hugeness of Spain dissolving into the endless horizon, all in a building as guarded as any fortress, keeping others out, keeping Spain in.

El Escorial was only one of Philip's many palaces and in fact he spent very little time there – but then, as now, its symbolic role and presence spreads right out across the Iberian Peninsula and down through the centuries, remaining as potent as ever.

Opposite: The soft stone and shadows of the cloisters are a brief respite from the overwhelming, monumental scale of the building.

Overleaf: The gardens move out from the building in increasing informality, starting with the tightly controlled, absolutely flat parterres, then the gently sloping orchards on the next layer, fields beyond that and then the wooded hunting grounds.

The garden is created from a very limited palette of plants that create a stunning combination of simplicity and subtlety.

Dehesa de Yonte
ÁVILA

'You will love Ávila,' they said. 'Lots of good restaurants in the old town. Great atmosphere.' Except that the only place to stay was a modern hotel some kilometres outside the city, situated in the middle of an industrial estate by the edge of a motorway. Vast atrium. Glass lifts. Key cards that never work last thing at night. A lot of gym activity too early in the morning. The desperate, solitary breakfasts of middle-aged men on the road missing their families. You know the kind of place.

Ávila itself – lovely old-town Ávila – had been glimpsed in the last light with its turreted city walls wrapped around by highways and swathes of new high-rise apartments. This was all en route to a garden about five kilometres north of the city, above the banks of the reservoir Castro de las Cogotas, called Dehesa de Yonte.

Turning off the main road, you bounce down a stone track flanked by huge boulders, the occasional holm oak and very little else. Anything that grows or lives here has to be very tough indeed. Ávila is the highest provincial capital in Spain and the garden is set at over 1,100 metres. It is blasted by heat in summer and by freezing temperatures in winter. The soil is thin to the point of emaciation. None of this makes for the ideal conditions for a garden of any kind. It is bleak.

But go through the gates to the drive leading to the house and you are immediately stopped in your tracks by the easy sophistication and sheer beauty of the garden. I hate the expression 'wow factor' but Dehesa de Yonte has just that. It stops you in your tracks. Wow. Blimey. Things are ratcheted up a notch or two. You could turn at the entrance and never come back and know that you have loved it.

Entrances are an underplayed element of gardens. There is often a modesty, even a coyness about them, so that you are expected to wander in, find the centre and perfect spot, let it wrap around you

before it reveals itself. But that first impression here is so dramatic and so powerful that it sets the tone and the key with which to unlock the rest of the garden.

Either side of the drive, laid in granite sets, there is a flowing combination of carefully clipped shrubs – lavender, phillyrea, rosemary, box – rising up through slim cypresses and carefully positioned olive trees. There are no hedges, no planted structure other than the trees. The palette is muted, pared down to soft greens, drifting from the dark green of the phillyrea through glaucous tones to the pale mauve of perovskia flowers. *Euphorbia characias* is clipped after flowering to make perfect tight mounds of smoky blue. A few gauras, of the palest pink, drift like a swarm of insects over the clipped shrubs. Although the planting, controlled as it is, is fluid, it is set against a series of stone walls made from nearby quarries, forming terraces, their horizontal precision and exact tones of the local stone dissolving into the fragmented rocks and boulders beyond the garden's edge.

The garden is now entering its eighth year and has reached the kind of maturity that gives it a sense of permanence. It defines itself by what it is now rather than any lingering potential. Having said that, the gardens of the very rich can bypass the embryonic stages by planting mature trees and

An open gravel area intended specifically for entertaining large parties has self-sown grasses, but the olives and clipped phillyrea domes had to be planted into holes blasted into solid rock.

shrubs and commissioning elaborate landscaping. To some extent that has happened here, but only up to a point – and that point was critical.

The garden was designed and made by the Urquijo-Kastner partnership. Miguel Urquijo – a distant cousin of Piru Urquijo at Los Molinillos – is in charge of the design and planting, and his wife, Renata Kastner, oversees and manages the projects. They work as a tight team and have established themselves as one of Spain's leading landscape architects with over 300 projects completed. However, initially they turned down the chance to make a garden here.

Miguel Urquijo showed me round the garden and explained that he was first asked to create a typical Mediterranean garden on what was then a bare site surrounding a derelict building. But when he inspected it, he knew that even if it was feasible, it was certainly not sustainable.

'There was nothing here – just a few boulders and dusty soil. In summer it is often over 40 degrees and in winter minus 15 for weeks on end. Mediterranean plants cannot survive in these conditions. So I said no.'

However, the owner returned to him and asked him to make what he could – with one proviso: there had to be olive trees. But that was very difficult. It is too cold for olives here.

'If you look around,' Miguel pointed out, 'there are none growing in the area.' But the holm oaks on the hillside had exactly the colour of olives and Miguel realised that the colour, if nothing else, was a key to work from. After much research, he found a strain of olives in Aragon, in the north of Spain, where the winters are equally cold. So he ordered mature specimens of this particular olive tree and, despite his initial misgivings, they have survived and their foliage is a linking harmony to the oaks on the hillside.

'But there was no soil to plant them. That is why I made the terraces, using the local stone for the walls and infilling with imported topsoil – so there was something to plant into.' In the gravelled area around the side of the house, designed specifically for entertaining large parties, the olives were planted by excavating pits in the solid rock.

Although he planted a range of shrubby plants – rosemary, phillyrea, lavender, box, rhamnus, osmanthus, ligustrum – Miguel has become a devoted fan of phillyrea as the one plant that thrives in this environment. The original planting has now made sizeable mounds, tightly – and extremely skilfully – clipped and seemingly impervious to the limitations of soil and climate, whilst almost everything else either struggles or needs replacing regularly.

As for replacements and initial planting, Miguel resists any instant gratification. 'I always plant from plugs. They grow faster, stronger and adapt better.' Every gardener sooner or later learns this, but it takes a steely resolve and some patience to put it into practice – especially when dealing with clients used to having their whims indulged in a hurry.

The one concession to whims and fancies is the lawn around the side of the house overlooking the reservoir. A large pine, one of the few trees originally here, dominates the very green sward. The two huge house mastiffs were stretched out and luxuriating in its shade. Miguel looked slightly bashful as he explained that it is primarily for the client's daughter to play on, accepting that it runs counter to the purer ethos of sustainability in all the other planting.

One of the very few original plants was this huge pine at the edge of the garden, casting much-needed shade.

We talked about the limitations of this kind of gardening. Does he miss being able to expand the range of plants here? No. It is self-defining. You work within these limitations as absolutes. Then Miguel said something that I have been thinking about ever since: 'You know, the problem with many British gardens is that they are spoilt by plants.'

I asked, eyebrow and perhaps horticultural hackles raised, what he means by this.

'You are like horticultural billionaires. Your climate is so mild and your soil so good that you can have and grow whatever you want. But this means that too many of your gardens are stuffed with too many plants and especially too wide a range. Gardening in a climate and soil like most of Spain's forces a gardener to select very carefully and think hard about how to grow. This is a useful discipline.'

He is right, of course. All good design is about editing. What is not there is as critical to the result as what remains. Dehesa de Yonte has a very limited range of plants, grown and tended in a limited way for very particular and limited effect. And it is marvellous. The subtlety of it is incredibly satisfying. The overriding lesson is to work with the limitations of the site – however extreme – and to have the confidence to be simple.

Above: The lawn is an unexpected and atypical splash of green and unsustainable in the climate but maintained explicitly for the owners' daughter to play on.

Opposite: The interweaving curves of beautifully shaped phillyrea and escallonia lapping about the trunk of an olive create movement and harmony with the simplest – but completely sustainable – of planting schemes.

Overleaf: The swimming pool had to be hacked out of the solid rock that most of the garden is made from and upon, and which provides the perfect backdrop.

The house at La Lancha is set in and amongst an olive grove but olives and oaks trees were moved near the house, given a pedestal of tightly clipped teucrium and set in mown grass to create the domestic centre from which the garden quickly spreads out into agricultural informality.

La Lancha
JARANDILLA DE LA VERA

RISING UP THROUGH FIELDS OF BLACK BULLS WITH HORNS AN ARMSPAN WIDE, THE ROAD WEST to Jarandilla de la Vera takes you over the mountain passes in the Parque Regional de la Sierra de Gredos, then down into Extremadura. Brick barns dot the fields, all similar in design and construction. They are tall and honeycombed with ventilation gaps in the brickwork, unlike any agricultural buildings I had seen anywhere else in the world. It turns out that this was the centre of the Spanish tobacco growing area and they are for drying tobacco. The uniformity of these buildings goes back to the Franco era when the industry was state controlled, although now hardly any tobacco is grown and if the barns are used at all it is to smoke paprika peppers over oak fires to make the distinctive feature of the region's cuisine.

After a night in a hotel in the small town of Jarandilla de la Vera, that had the feeling of an out-of-season ski resort, we drove a few kilometres out of town, then down a long track through uncultivated countryside, the rich, musty smell from the previous night's rain rising from the earth and cattle lurching out of the mist from the bracken, square bells around their necks clanging. This is the road to the Finca La Lancha, which belongs to Eduardo Mencos and his wife, Anneli. Both have extensively photographed and written about gardens all over Spain, but their own garden is unusual in that it exists in the liminal space between garden and farm.

Move up just a little from the fertile valley and the land is wilder, bigger, bleaker. Beyond the hills rising into the clouds in the west is the Portuguese border. Whereas Ávila feels commutable, connected to the capital, this feels a long way and completely separate from Madrid.

The track became an olive grove and led to the finca where Eduardo and Anneli were waiting. She, dark eyed and direct, he a lumbering bear of a man, and both warm and welcoming. An enormous

Sheep graze under the olives and are allowed into the garden to act as mowers.

deerhound, a mastiff, a dachshund and a collie accompanied us as we went through a gate into the garden, which is pressed about the house, trees growing up through clipped box. A sunken vegetable plot leads off to one side, with pink-rendered, chunky raised beds and, round the corner, a swimming pool in the shape of a cross. Everything is shaded by climbers and the spreading branches of trees planted to that end, everything tightly domestic and certainly not treading into any kind of agricultural territory.

But the finca runs to 30 hectares (75 acres) and the garden opens out behind the house. An avenue of holm oaks and cypresses cut through an olive grove and run down to a distant large rock – the *lancha*, or 'boat', that gives the place its name – erupting from the open field. The grass is tightly mown, partly, it turns out, by sheep that periodically graze, and partly by a robot mower. It is an interesting and unlikely combination but perhaps a good picture of the deliberate horticultural hybrid of farm and garden.

Eduardo was explicit about this. He set out to create a modern *ferme ornée*, based upon the eighteenth-century Arcadian model, first described by Stephen Switzer in 1715 and practised most notably in the UK at Woburn Farm in the 1740s and The Leasowes in Halesowen by William Shenstone in the 1750s. It never really took off or caught the public's imagination but was the forerunner of the landscape gardens made by Capability Brown and later, Humphry Repton, and of the concept of a park and farm as being a place of leisure, pleasure and beauty.

To this end, Eduardo has moved oak trees, olives and cypresses from around the farm, all done with his old tractor, to create vistas and walks. He planted a thick, tightly clipped collar of teucrium around the bases of these transplants. This adds formality, contrasting with the looser shapes of the surrounding olives – although these too are pruned carefully every year. He told me that nothing has been cut down – everything moved has been replanted and is surviving.

A line of olives has been placed on a mound in a field containing an amorous donkey, their trunks stained mahogany russet. These too are repurposed and repositioned. The trees having been moved and the avenue cleared, distant mountains now draw the eye out effortlessly and there is nothing to distract or offend in the middle ground between the finca and that dramatic horizon.

A hard jangle of tinny bells announced the arrival of a large flock of sheep, belonging to Eduardo's neighbour, for a brief munch of the grass under the olives. It was obviously a display put on especially for us and one not often repeated. The ground was suspiciously clear of droppings before their appearance and, as one who has kept sheep for years, I know just how much poo they leave in their wake and how long it sticks around for. But the point is made. They can and do co-exist with the garden, albeit in this case for just 15 minutes or so before the robot mower takes over grazing duties.

After the flock had moved on to pastures new, the next agricultural display arrived in the shape of a team to harvest olives from the grove. They spread out nets around the tree and then one of them started up what looked like a hedge cutter on a long pole, but instead of a cutting blade had a hook that vibrated the branches. Others whacked at the fruit with long canes, causing fruit and leaves to tumble into the nets. All the trees would have this treatment in due course and their olives would be pressed to make the year's supply of a particularly fruity oil for the household.

Although the landscape is both fierce and magnificent, the climate is wetter than the more central Ávila and Madrid, with rain from the Atlantic coming over the hills and dropping down on this side. 'We have more rain than in London,' Eduardo told me. 'But when it comes, it comes very strongly, with a lot of passion. Like everything in Spain.'

There has certainly been a lot of passion, energy and skill gone into making the garden, but an important measure of subtlety too. 'The work should remain underground,' is how Eduardo put it, so you should be admiring not the labour or ambition but the results. It means that garden and farmland and landscape should merge into each other without any noticeable jolt or division, save perhaps the smaller areas right around the house.

They are working from a good base. The olive groves here, as everywhere, are innately and effortlessly handsome in a domesticated fashion, especially when growing in an ordered, well-pruned grid out of sheep-grazed grass. And if the sheep become too agriculturally messy then there is always the robot mower to keep the sward neat and even.

Below: The olives are harvested by knocking and shaking them from the branches into nets spread out on the ground below.

Opposite: Eduardo Mencos has planted cypresses amongst the olives, incorporating garden and farm in a seamless integration.

Previous spread: Spain produces more wine than any other country and the Douro Valley is dominated by mile upon mile of vineyards.

Opposite: Peter Sissek's very modern, Danish-designed home sits on a slope above his experimental garden that overlooks the Douro Valley.

Alnardo
VALLADOLID

It is a long drive from La Lancha, back over the mountains to Ávila and on through the seemingly endless flat reaches of León to Valladolid. Again and again, the sheer size and scale of Spain is overwhelming, although much of this particular journey was done in the dark and we finally arrived at a hotel attached to a winery, the only indication of which was the smell of fermenting grapes. But dawn and drawn curtains revealed vineyards stretching to the horizon. Spain is the largest wine producer in the world and this, the Douro Valley, a few kilometres east of Valladolid, is the centre of that largess, with bodegas and wineries lining the roads, separated only by more vineyards.

In a sense, it is wine that brought us here. Peter Sisseck has become famous for producing one of the most exclusive and expensive wines in Spain with, when I last looked, his Pingus wine selling at around £1,500 a bottle. The small vineyard growing the grapes for this liquid treasure is a few kilometres down the road but I was there to visit Peter's own garden, set on a hill above the Douro Valley. I had heard about it from Tom Stuart-Smith who had worked on it with Peter. It was, Tom said, the most inhospitable site for a garden he had known. What do you mean by that? I had asked. 'Go and see,' Tom said. So here I was, coming to see.

Peter's house sits halfway up the south-facing hillside, the plateau on the far side of the plain as flat-topped as a 1950s GI's haircut. The house is a modern and very handsome interlocking series of white stone rectangles. Big glass windows reveal stylish and sleek minimalist furniture and white stone paths link to a pool and gym building, with mounds of rosemary softening all those straight edges and lines. So far, so predictable – if very well executed – for the home of a very successful and stylish person. But – and it is a whopping great but – the hillside below the house challenges every conception of what a garden is, could be or perhaps even should be.

Like so much of inland Spain, the conditions are, to say the least, demanding. The garden is 850 metres above sea level, has very low rainfall and a huge variation between the extremes of heat in summer and cold in winter. The soil is thin and almost devoid of nutrients. But instead of trying to improve the conditions, Peter decided to work with them and take the garden and its planting to its logical and literal extremes. So he contacted Tom Stuart-Smith and Professor James Hitchmough for advice, the former having a reputation as one of the leading landscape designers working with natural planting within gardens, and the latter an academic who has led the way with research into horticultural ecology at the University of Sheffield.

 In 2015, Tom and his team planted 15,000 plants into the site, which is about one and half hectares or just under four acres. All were natives, mostly found on the hillside around the finca. Within a few years, at least half had died. Peter has added another 5,000 plants since then – all propagated in the little nursery that he has set up from existing plants on the hillside around.

It quickly became obvious that Peter, although urbane and relaxed in manner, wants to push the experiment as far as it can go and he is prepared to do whatever it takes to that end. Under that easy-going exterior is great focus and intensity. You can see how his wines have become so renowned.

What you see now is a hillside dotted thinly with scrubby, scruffy plants. The herbaceous plants had been strimmed back a few days before so there was no dead vegetation, but an awful lot of what looked like fairly dead ground between the plants. On closer inspection, though, this soil proved to be neither bare nor dead but holding quite a few seedlings, albeit tiny and clearly clinging on to life. Nearer the top of the hillside and the house, santolina and rosemary seemed very happy and had formed established low mounds. Euphorbia has adapted well and is spread widely, if not thickly.

Why, I asked Peter, try to make a garden on what must be the least suitable site in Europe? Why bother to even try to make a garden here and fight nature?

'That,' Peter politely rebuked me, 'is the wrong mindset. We are not fighting nature but going with it. We are just trying to find out what nature needs on this site and that means a lot of trial and error. It is a good laboratory.'

That is the key to this garden. It is an experiment.

As it happens, down the hillside, tucked in amongst the holm oaks, is a large and conventional kitchen garden producing masses of vegetables – along with the immaculately kept chickens and beef cattle, existing solely to produce dung, which is mixed with grape skins and vine prunings to make compost for the biodynamic vines and vegetable garden. Next to them is the greenhouse where a couple of young men are taking cuttings. And next to that, banks of solar panels, which supply all the electricity. Everything here is linked and part of the bigger experiment in living as much as in gardening.

The seedlings are the essence of the site's sustainability. Whilst parent plants, even of perennials, may not be able to live longer than a season, if they can produce seed then they not only continue to inhabit the site but also create a breeding programme, whereby those that survive best and set most seed for longest will gradually evolve strains best adapted to the location – and Peter said that after eight years, this is already happening. Along with taking cuttings from the successful shrubs, he is

Whereas the garden around the house is an experiment in non-intervention and native plants, the vegetable garden, further down the hillside, is a model of order and productivity.

developing an ecology perfectly adapted to the place. The downside, in conventional horticultural terms, is that it is a case of survival of the fittest. The plant base becomes reduced to the thugs – or to put it more politely, those that adapt best. There is no room for the marginal or slightly temperamental, thus excluding a wide range of potentially delightful plants.

But Peter was unapologetic about this. The whole point of the experiment is to create a garden that has true resilience to the location – let alone the growing restrictions imposed by climate change. The range of plants might be very limited but that has never stopped beautiful and rewarding gardens being made, and of all the gardeners I have ever met around the world, he is the one that I am sure will carry this through to its sustainable conclusion.

Whereas at La Lancha they are making a garden that merges into farm without any apparent division or boundary, Peter is creating a liminal space sitting somewhere between garden and completely natural hillside. But I don't think that there is any of the kind of moral crusade that accompanies more self-conscious 'rewilding'. He has the resources to make any kind of garden that he wants, but for Peter, the beauty and rewards of this garden come with the experiment of working in an uncompromising fashion with the natural conditions and its harsh rhythms.

In gardening terms, there is a simplicity and inevitability about this that every gardener comes to sooner or later, even if most of us resist it by continuing to grow a range of plants that need a great deal of mollycoddling to survive. Peter is simply following the most important axiom of any garden, that of finding the right plant for the right place. He just happens to be doing it in one of the most horticulturally demanding places you might possibly conceive.

Palacio de Galiana
TOLEDO

FROM VALLADOLID, WHICH IS AS FAR NORTH AS THIS LEG OF THE JOURNEY TOOK ME, I SWEPT back south, through Ávila, past Madrid, on down to Toledo, arriving at dusk, the Alcázar and medieval walls lit up like Christmas lights.

The next morning, I discovered that the view from my balcony reached across the soft pink stone of the gorge that drops down to the Tagus River as it curves around the old town, taking in terracotta roofs and the greeny-blue haze of olive leaves scattered across the slopes.

Toledo's history is long, exalted and troubled. Occupied in turn by Romans, Visigoths and Moors, it was the main palace of Charles V and a Nationalist rebel stronghold for Franco's troops in the Civil War. As well as being the home of El Greco and the manufacture of the best swords and daggers in Europe, Toledo was the centre for botanical studies in Al-Andalus and in the eleventh century had one of the first botanical gardens.

A mile or so outside the city, the Palacio de Galiana was first built by the Berber leader Al-Mamun towards the end of the eleventh century as a summer pavilion right next to the Tagus, to escape the heat of the city. It was then taken over by a succession of rulers after the Moors were driven from Toledo at the end of the century and the surviving building is based upon the ruins of the thirteenth-century pavilion built on the site by Alfonso X.

The name is based upon the story of Galiana, daughter of the Muslim king Galafre in Toledo, who became the wife of Emperor Charlemagne, converting to Christianity in the process. This predates the original building by two centuries, but the story and the name has stuck. The building became a monastery for a while, was sold by the monks and passed through a series of private hands down the centuries until, by the twentieth century, palace and gardens had become badly neglected.

In 1959, it was purchased by Alejandro Fernández de Araoz and his wife Carmen Marañón – who was the mother of Piru Urquijo at Los Molinillos. They restored the palace to its present state to be used as a place for concerts, lectures and parties, rather than as a home, and after her husband's death in 1970, Carmen Marañón spent most of her time living there in a small house that they built in the grounds, restoring building and garden until her own death in 2005.

The garden suffered badly in the exceptionally cold weather of January 2021 brought by Storm Filomena. Olive trees and palms died and a number of cypresses were broken by the sheer weight of snow. But plenty of pencil-slim cypresses remain, planted by Carmen, along with roses, pelargoniums in terracotta pots hanging from the wall and a *charbagh* of sorts, delineated in paths laid in herringbone fashion with slim bricks, centred upon a small, bubbling fountain. This nod to the palace's Islamic origins is made all the stronger for the unglazed windows.

The building is part enormous garden pavilion and part immaculately maintained ruin. With its

Above: At the back of the building a lower floor – once ceilinged over – now houses a pond and the walls are lined with ranks of terracotta pots filled with prostrate rosemary.

Opposite: The slim green columns of cypresses beautifully balance the horizontal courses of pink stone.

beautifully restored Mudejar plasterwork, it honours its Moorish heritage, and the horseshoe and polylobed arches perfectly frame every view of the garden. That it is not used for daily domestic life – no bathrooms, kitchens or any designated rooms at all, just spaces that are grand and satisfying with a few carefully chosen and simple pieces of furniture – is inspiring and exhilarating, freeing up preconceptions of how one automatically uses buildings. It has been treasured and restored for what it is, not for how it might be used.

Outside, where a courtyard might be expected to be, is a two-storey drop, with a square, very shallow pond at the base, the thin film of water catching light and bouncing it back up onto the arcaded, ivy-filled walls to the scores of pots standing rim to rim and all spilling over with prostrate rosemary. The pale terracotta of the walls, the pots and stone of the palace, all echo the same shades of pale pink and burnt orange, with the ivy, rosemary and cypress blocking in walls of green. It is very simple but quietly effective, and all part of the seductive stage set of palace and garden, waiting for the actors to arrive.

Overleaf: The building – like Toledo itself – has a strong Islamic heritage, reflected in the beautifully restored and elaborately decorated Mudejar arches of the unglazed windows.

The dramatic brick stairway down from the house, lined by walls of cypresses, has a rill running down its centre, stopping at small square pools and fountains on its landings before entering the canal at the bottom.

Las Nieves
TOLEDO

On the outskirts of Toledo, on a hillside of olives on otherwise rocky, barren ground, is a former monastery. It was built in 1480 and remained an active religious centre until Napoleon's troops arrived in 1808, threw out the monks, used the buildings as a barracks and pillaged the site. In the 1830s after the Peninsular War (or, as the Spanish know it, the War of Independence) the land and surviving buildings were sold to private owners as part of the great dispersal of ecclesiastical land of the mid-nineteenth century.

So it remained, passing from owner to owner until the current family bought it in 1945. For 40 years it was used as a hunting lodge with most of the monastic buildings broken ruins and heaps of rubble smothered in vegetation. Then, in the mid-1980s, it was decided to excavate and shore them up. Pictures taken before the work began show the extent of the restoration that has taken place, transforming what looked like a bombsite to a beautifully restored structure with a garden that stands comparison to Fountains or Tintern Abbey in Britain.

The landscape architect Leandro Silva was commissioned to begin a garden around the ruins. He moved huge, gnarled, sinewy olives from the hillside of the estate and created a double avenue underplanted with rosemary leading to the front door. It immediately sets the tone of grandeur and drama, yet using the vernacular of the landscape. He also designed the huge brick stairway leading down from the back of the house. This was put into effect by the architect restoring the buildings, who also made the water maze to one side of the entrance.

The brick staircase is both conceptually and structurally astonishing. You come through the internal courtyard to a covered veranda, where most of the living is clearly done, and which opens out onto a steep drop down four long flights of steps. A rill runs down the middle, with a square fountain on each

of the three landings as well as at the base, before emptying into a long canal below. Both sides of this huge brick stairway are flanked by tall cypresses rising up in green walls of 10 to 15 metres high.

For all its drama, it is very simple in concept and content. Green walls, narrow terracotta bricks and pale grey mortar joints almost as wide as the bricks themselves. The rill a straight groove running like a glistening fault line between the square basins that are exactly the same width as the canal – everything lined up and linear and heading fiercely out. It is outrageously effective.

The steps with their integrated water are Islamic in style, but at the far end of the canal, and the funnelled focus of this dramatic stage, is a sixteenth-century crucifix, apparently taken from a crossroads, conflating and colliding cultures and religions. Carved into the base is a scallop shell, so it may well have come from the Camino de Santiago.

At the bottom of the steps, turn right and the main building is high above you on a slope covered with bay, cypress, myrtle and a little box – in fact, the entire planting throughout the garden consists of little more than these four plants. I was told that this was the essence of Castilian gardening – no

Above: The planting within the monastic buildings is strong but restrained and follows the rhythm of the arches of the building.

Opposite: At the end of the canal at the foot of the steep brick stairway with its strong debt to Islamic design is a sixteenth-century crucifix, apparently taken from a crossroads, conflating and colliding cultures and religions.

Overleaf: A labyrinth planted in bay replaced the original, which was destroyed in the great snowstorm of 2021, and is already becoming established.

flowers, no fragrance, just green. Ahead is a large double parterre made of two sets of four beds laid out in bay. This was destroyed by the great snows of 2021 and has had to be replanted but was growing strongly when I visited.

So far so dramatic and strong, but turn right again and back towards the building, through a stone arch set in ivy-covered walls, and the drama increases tenfold, because now you enter into the cloisters and nave of the monastery, beautifully cleared and restored, and holding the green of a garden. It is an extraordinary experience to walk through a garden amongst this scale of buildings, with its proportion of stone to green that no modern garden could possibly replicate.

The design and maintenance doubles down on this relationship and resists every temptation for horticultural embellishment. There is green grass in the nave, green ivy on the walls – carefully clipped and controlled so as not to soften or obscure the architectural details – large, tightly clipped bay domes and smaller box balls and that is it. It is more than enough. The floors of the cloisters around the outside are paved with beautiful recycled flagstones, so stone floors rise seamlessly into

Thirty-two ancient olive trees have been moved from the surrounding groves of the estate to form a gnarled and venerable avenue approaching the house.

By restricting the colour inside the monastic ruins to green and resisting any horticultural complexity, the garden assumes real power and presence with the ruins rather than being a garden inside them.

stone walls topped by sky, when there must have been the temptation to make these cloisters grass too. More would clutter and diminish the grandeur and beautiful simplicity that has reduced the garden down to essence and the building to a noble ghost, and from the combination made a sublime synthesis.

There is a water labyrinth to be found up and beyond the ruined area, and various seating places with a few roses, but to be honest, they feel like peripheral, albeit admirable, horticultural exercises and are inevitably overwhelmed by the majestic symphony playing within the ragged walls.

I suspect that it takes the extremes of climate coupled with the inherent pride and ferocity that is deep in the blood of Spanish culture to create a garden that is so reduced to its elemental bones and yet so rich in drama, history and physical grandeur.

I am often asked the question 'what is a Spanish garden?'. Although I suspect that a clear, true answer is as unachievable as defining Spain itself, I am certain that this garden could not, would not, have been made anywhere but in Spain.

Opposite: Watching and waiting by one of the beautifully ornate front doors.

Below: A stone drinking trough in the central courtyard makes a modern water feature in tune with the simplicity and power of the restored monastic buildings.

Monforte Gardens
VALENCIA

THE MONFORTE GARDENS WERE CREATED WHEN THE MARQUÉS DE SAN JUAN BOUGHT A vegetable plot in the middle of the city in 1849 and commissioned a large garden attached to the handsome villa he built. For the next 20 years, he planted and collected plants, especially trees, and the garden developed into maturity. He had no children, so when he died in 1872, he left the house and garden to the children of his niece and it remained in the Monforte family for the next hundred years until the council bought the gardens in 1971, restored them and opened them to the public in 1974.

Much of the garden remains unaltered since its nineteenth-century heyday and in 1941 it was declared a National Artistic Garden by the Service for the Defence of National Artistic Heritage, formed by Franco's government after the Civil War with the brief 'to reorganise the protection of the national artistic heritage and protect it from the events of war, the destructive fury and the acquisitive improvision of mobs, governments and other forms of pillage seen during the red resistance'. Whatever the political morality involved in this, in the case of Monforte, it led to sensitive restoration and meant that a remarkable, untouched example of a nineteenth-century romantic garden remains, despite the modern blocks that encircle it and which would otherwise almost certainly have taken over the site.

To have a well-preserved garden so specifically of a period, which was private for so many years now open free of charge to visitors every day of the year, is rare. When I went, it had a steady flow of mainly young visitors, none of whom displayed the self-conscious garden awareness that so characterises visitors in Britain to National Trust gardens. It seemed that it was just a nice place to drop into on a hot, busy day – and if you did not know the name of any plants or relate the style and design to any period, then that lack of knowledge or curiosity made it no less pleasant.

However, there is much that is fascinating if you are interested in garden history because there are few gardens of this period that have survived the twentieth century more or less unaltered.

The garden is roughly divided into three. There is a large and complicated parterre near the house planted with box and myrtle from which marble statues of classical figures rise. A central rose garden around a large bay tree, retaining all the characteristics associated with nineteenth-century formal planting, with hybrid tea roses set in bare soil, and at the far end of the site a wilderness along with what are now large, mature trees from the original planting. The wilderness has an understory of fatsia, monstera and large howea underplanted in turn with the strappy leaves of clivia, all of which throws the northern, park association of the roses completely askew. It is a fascinating mixture.

A superb banksia rose covers one end wall near the house with clouds of primrose yellow flowers against the absolute blue of the sky – I always think of the banksia rose as a tantalising measure of a benign climate as I long to grow it at home but know it would never survive even the mildest of our own winters.

Above: Classical statues frame a portal leading down steps to a small courtyard and a circular pond off the side of the villa.

Opposite: A hedge cut in gentle swoops separates the formal rose garden from the loose green of the wilderness.

In the early 1970s, when the garden was first opened to the public, a new area to one side was laid out consisting of euonymus hedges bounding borders filled with *Hydrangea macrophylla*, the nod towards modernity made via a backing hedge varying from the rest of the rigorously horizontal lines by undulating in regular waves. It is probably much enjoyed by visitors but feels unnecessary, like a modern room in a house that is otherwise Victorian in every detail.

Monforte is a garden of paths, all leading to what seems an indeterminate goal as they are flanked by tall hedges of cypress and yew and pass under large, fully mature trees that close down any view. Many of these trees are part of the original planting and listed as *arbre monumental* – exceptionally good and large examples. So there is *Phoenix canariensis*, the Canary palm, a huge gingko, a Japanese plum yew, *Cephalotaxus harringtonia*, which, unlike the British *Taxus baccata*, has edible fruit but is equally slow growing. All this amounts to delicious shade in a city that, in April, was already hot and obviously going to get much hotter over the summer months.

Overleaf: The villa opens out onto a parterre of clipped euonymus with statues in white Carrara marble. In the background the yellow flowers of *Rosa banksiae* are in full bloom.

Palms and pines grow on what was once the bed of the Turia River and grass and paths run between the exposed arches of the bridge.

Turia Park

VALENCIA

FROM TOLEDO, DERRY AND I WENT TO ARANJUEZ, INTENDING TO SEE PHILIP II'S PALACE GARDENS there. We travelled in a wild hooley of a storm, roads flooded, traffic backed up for many kilometres, driving bonnet deep through puddles. The next morning was bright and clear, the storm blown over, but so too were many trees in the royal gardens and it was indeterminately closed. So we crossed that off our list and pushed on to the final destination, right across the centre of the country, until we reached Valencia and the Mediterranean coast.

The region around Valencia is one of the most fertile in the whole of Spain. The soil is good and the Albufera wetlands to the south of the city grow the rice for paella, which, despite being generally associated with Spain by most tourists in the way that bacon and eggs is British or pasta Italian, belongs distinctly and specifically to Valencia.

Whilst the ingredients of a paella are not specific nor constant, ranging from rabbit and chicken to seafood, green beans, butter beans, paprika, tomato and always rice, the absolute non-negotiable element for Valencians is the use of the local, particularly hard, chalky water, and Valencian water, or the absence of it, is the key to the hugely ambitious park created in the middle of the city.

The Turia River ran right through the middle of the city but over the centuries was prone to flooding, often with lethal and very destructive effect. In October 1957, there was the last of these catastrophic floods, the water rising to two metres in parts of the city, resulting in the deaths of over 80 people and nearly 6,000 homes destroyed, with almost total loss of all commercial activity. Enough was enough. So the decision was made to reroute the river south of the city. This was completed by 1970, leaving a ten-kilometre stretch of dry riverbed running right through the centre, which, the council decided, would be ideal for a sunken motorway that linked the airport and docks

Left: The best way to get about along the ten-kilometre length of the park is by bicycle.

Opposite: There are 18 bridges spanning the park dating from medieval times to the twentieth century, all now to be appreciated as bridges rarely are, fully exposed, their buttresses rising from dry ground.

Overleaf: The park currently ends with the magnificent architecture of the City of Arts and Sciences, although it will eventually continue to the port.

to the heart of the city. But there was such furious local opposition to the prospect of the river becoming a six-lane highway mainlining pollutants and noise and stress into centre of the city's life that people power won the day; by 1979, the original scheme was abandoned and replaced by a plan to make a huge urban park running along the riverbed.

The first thing that strikes you when you stand on one of the 18 bridges across the park is how deep and wide it is – an average of 200 metres from bank to bank. It is as though the Thames in the centre of London was to empty. It is a big space. The second thing is that this great sinuous length of green freeway right through the centre of a modern city is an outrageously simple but brilliant concept, and almost certainly could not have happened without the upwelling of people power. Apparently, the strength of feeling and unity of voice was irresistible. This is the people's park and that has set the tone of every aspect of it.

Work began on this in the early 1980s with a masterplan by the Catalan architect Ricardo Bofill involving 18 different sections, each with their own designer. To date, all but one of these 18 sections has been completed and ranges from sports grounds and formal gardens to the astonishing City of Arts and Sciences. Although the scale and ambition of the project was huge, it was much less expensive than building a motorway would have been.

Once you go down to riverbed level, it is surprising how quiet it is. Busy roads run either side but you can scarcely hear them. People sit quietly meditating, reading and chatting in the green shade. Runners run and a unicyclist nonchalantly weaves through people walking to work. For all the peaceful atmosphere it generates, it is clearly an important artery within the city – quicker, easier and more pleasant than driving or cycling on the streets above.

The creation of the park seems to have inspired and encouraged the city authorities to do all that they can to make Valencia as environmentally sustainable as possible and, in their own words, the greenest city in Europe. I met José Ignacio Lacomba, who is responsible for sustainable gardening at the city council. He said that they intended to make Valencia carbon neutral by 2025 and that one of the less expected but valuable effects of the park was that it greatly increased people's health. Many people lived near enough to use it daily and there had been an upsurge of running, walking and team sports. On top of that, the mental health benefits of having green spaces accessible to all were very important. It began life, he said, as a result of the irresistible demands of the people of Valencia and remains open and inclusive to all the citizens.

One of the side effects of diverting the river is that the bridges take on a different role. Some remain for traffic but many are now pedestrianised, so have become part of the project rather than a way of getting past or over it. They take you to tree level where the parakeets noisily rush to and from their nests and the mauve flowers of the false acacias are heavy with fragrance.

The pedestrian Bridge of Flowers, built in 2003, was completely decked in thousands of pelargoniums in every shade of lipstick pink when I visited in mid-April, a dense hedge of garish flower above the modern concrete sides, beneath a row of palms rising up from the riverbed below. Garish, but fun and celebratory, and very busy at eight in the morning.

From the ground, the arches of the sixteenth-century Puente de Serranos, with their buttresses sharply angled into the waters of centuries past, have beautiful clean, sculptural lines, which ordinarily would never be seen. You realise that we see most bridges from above or sideways and to stand on the ground looking up at them, grass running under the arches where river once flowed, is a rare treat.

As far as the individual gardens or sections of the park go, no one area is particularly exceptional in any conventional horticultural way. But that is not the point. It is the scale of imagination and execution, the sheer heft of the concept that makes it so special. It is an unalloyed success story. The people of Valencia chose it, use it and clearly love it.

One of the features of the park, with mature trees growing freely along its length, is how insulated it is from the noise of the surrounding city. As well as being the best way of moving around from west to east and having many sports pitches and facilities, it is also full of places for quiet relaxation.

SOUTHERN SPAIN

La Fortaleza
MALLORCA

PORT DE POLLENÇA IS SET ALONG THE CURVE OF A DEEP BAY FLANKED BY OUTSTRETCHED promontories and on one the squat stone keep of Fortaleza still stands sentinel. It was begun in the 1620s and finally completed 70 years later to defend the then important port against Berber pirates, brigands and other unwelcome visitors. Pollença is at the trading crossroads of the Mediterranean and, in consequence, was often raided by pirates looking for booty. The fort has become a coveted wedding venue, film set – including locations for the BBC's *The Night Manager* – and holiday retreat for the very rich and famous, with two swimming pools, heliport, seven different buildings, private landing coves, terraced gardens and luxurious accommodation. Indeed, at one point in 2008, Fortaleza was sold as the most expensive private house in the whole of Spain.

The pirate threat had waned by the end of the nineteenth century and in 1919, the wealthy Argentinian painter Roberto Ramaugé bought and converted the fort, making the garden in the process. Throughout the 1920s and 1930s, Ramaugé used Fortaleza as a community for painters, who, drawn by the light, congregated in Pollença, and as a place to entertain and host his artistic friends, including Andrés Segovia and Pablo Picasso, with famously wild parties.

The Spanish Civil War put an abrupt end to this and in 1936 the fort was confiscated by the Spanish Air Force who used it as a base for sea planes. After the war, it slowly fell into disuse and disrepair before the Ramaugé family took back possession in 1984. They restored it and then sold it in 2008 for that ground-breaking sum. Ramaugé's garden was laid out on generous terraces with the glorious but almost absurdly theatrical swimming pool sitting below the late seventeenth-century octagonal fort like an ironic, surreal moat. In a few extraordinary places like this, a garden really does not have to do much to become a delight, with horticulture playing second fiddle to location.

Opposite: The stone facade around the pool frames the glorious blue of the Mediterranean, once the hunting ground of marauding pirates plundering Pollença but now attracting hordes of tourists.

Below: The fort has recently been extensively modernised and restored to become an exclusive wedding venue and celebrity hideout.

Steps flanked by clipped balls of
myrtle and date palms lead up to the
thirteenth-century main entrance.

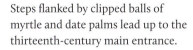

Alfabia
MALLORCA

THE ALFABIA GARDEN IS TUCKED UNDER THE BACKDROP OF THE TRAMUNTANA MOUNTAINS, inland and the other side from the towns of Deià and Sóller. These hillsides provide the water that is central to the garden's existence. The Moors, who took over Mallorca under the Emirate of Córdoba in the beginning of the tenth century, developed an irrigation system whereby the water from the mountains was channelled into *acequias* which could be tapped at any point so the pressure would bring a supply to the surface. The same system, installed over a thousand years ago, still operates at Alfabia.

The Moorish rule of Mallorca came to an end in 1229 but Islamic influence remains deep-seated in the island's culture, and the Alfabia Garden holds the central idea of the Islamic paradise of water, orchards and spring flowers all within a safe, enclosed space. In fact, what is most striking to the Eurocentric horticultural eye is the role that orchards play in this. We have come to see an orchard as something separate, relegated to the perimeter of the garden proper as a liminal agricultural space. Whereas at the Alfabia, and in all Islamic gardens, fruit trees were at the heart and centre of all planting.

You arrive at the original Moorish entrance gate via a long flight of steps climbing through the orchards with large-clipped myrtle balls at each rise. This was completely rebuilt in 1945 and the plane trees that formerly flanked the steps replaced by the current palms. At the top, to one side is an exquisite cistern, fed by mountain water, waist high and arched over by stone, the water shimmering jade with reflected light from the valley beyond.

Turn right at the gate and you face a long stone pergola heading down the slope set on stout round pillars and dressed with wisteria. This is an eighteenth-century addition added by the garden's

owner Gabriel de Berga y Zaforteza and, as it stands, it provides handsome shade to stroll beneath. However, its main entertainment value derives from the water games that were so popular in Renaissance and baroque Italian gardens. This consists here of a pressure pad that when stepped on by the unwitting visitor, triggers a cross fusillade of 24 jets running up each side, guaranteeing that anyone entering the length of the pergola will have a wetting. Fun and hilarity for all involved, except perhaps the guest with extra fine clothes.

Walking to the rear of the house between more citrus and apple orchards, the ground between the trees ploughed into corduroy rills with cereals and fruit grown in and amongst each other, you come to a nineteenth-century Romantic garden with a very different character. This is filled with an assortment of plants gathered from around the world, including palms, clivias, bamboos, eucalypts and monsteras planted around a series of pools. Whereas visitors walk up the steps and

Above: The garden is at the base of the Tramuntana mountains and created around the Islamic ideal of the paradise garden including and included within an orchard of dates, citrus, olives, pomegranates and figs.

Opposite: Looking across the flight of entrance steps, through the flattened cushions of myrtle and the arching fronds of the palms.

Overleaf: At the top of the steps, set to one side, is an exquisite cistern fed by mountain water, waist high and arched over by stone, the water shimmering jade with reflected light from the valley beyond.

down the pergola once, stopping to pose perhaps, shrieking a little at the triggered spray, admiring but not lingering, here in the cool green lushness, so different from the Mediterranean landscape around, the visiting public sit and eat ice creams, stop being diligent sightseers at a historical site and relax.

But this nineteenth-century addition, for all its botanical treasures and the way that the public clearly enjoys it, feels a sideshow to the combination of Moorish and baroque. And with its integration of the agricultural orchards and fields with the baroque garden, this earlier garden sits slightly uneasily with the modern eye, the whole too agriculturally scruffy and utilitarian juxtaposed with moments of sublimity. The whole too much at odds with its various parts. To conjoin these things and make them aesthetically pleasing for modern taste takes a particular Spanish garden design genius – and it was to one of his gardens that I went next, over on the other side of the island.

Left: The stone pergola is a baroque addition and with a very typical baroque joke, a series of 24 water jets soak the unsuspecting visitor when they step on a pressure pad.

Opposite: The garden at the rear of the house is influenced by English country gardens yet filled with a selection of tropical plants that were arriving into Europe in the late nineteenth century.

Cotoner was one of the first gardens by Fernando Caruncho to use the agricultural landscape as part of the garden rather than just as borrowed landscape, and the mown grass and cypresses sit within and around the cereal crop.

Cotoner

MALLORCA

THE ROAD FROM OUR HOTEL TO COTONER CROSSED THE FLAT CENTRE OF THE ISLAND, through early morning silver spring light, flashes of white stone walls, and gusts of orange blossom coming through the open car windows as we passed. The garden is approached by swinging round a field of wheat, hedged by a row of close-set cypresses but affording flickering glimpses of green beyond.

Cotoner was an early work by Fernando Caruncho and he is here with us, revisiting it with his son Pedro, having not seen it for many years.

I confess that I have long been in awe of his work – along with almost anybody who has had connections with garden design over the past 30 years. He is, for all his personal modesty, indisputably a master. I first met and got to know him – and Pedro – back in 2006. Fernando has barely changed over the years but Pedro was just 12 then and now is an established designer in his own right with a child of his own and working with his father, translating both language and ideas, and this was his first visit to Cotoner.

Cotoner was one of Caruncho's early gardens, made 30 years ago, and was one of the first to incorporate agricultural crops and orchards, integrating them just as the Moors did for thousands of years but with Caruncho adding his own confidence of line and rhythm that merges landscape into garden and garden into landscape.

The design at Cotoner, created around what was a finca surrounded by its flat, agricultural fields, is based upon a grid with square orchards of citrus, pomegranates, arbuteo, figs and wheat. There are also blocks of palms and olives. A large pond is in the centre and rows of clipped hedges ripple out from the water right up to the edge of the building like waves. The matrix of the grid is defined by exceptionally green, tightly mown grass, tying it all together, domesticating it and creating avenues

and sight lines. This is the Islamic paradise garden translated and re-formed through the lens of hundreds of years of assimilation, its influence still fundamental and potent – taking the *charbagh* with its central water and linking it to its agricultural surroundings – and yet comfortable with its modernity. It is a garden to be looked at from the veranda and walked in during the cool of the evening – a backdrop to life and never the life itself.

Fernando told me that there were four aspects he wanted to include – wheat, for the rhythm of the countryside; the Tramunanta mountains in the distance with the buildings and in particular the roof of the poolside hut; water, with the pond and the waves of the hedges; and Islamic tradition with the orchards.

The soil was originally very poor and for two years a leguminous crop was ploughed into the site to enrich the soil and to get bacterial activity into it. Then, he said, 'I planted small, very small, and this meant that everything adapted better and grew quicker as a result.'

Above all, he wanted to catch the rhythm of the agricultural year and every stage of it, from cultivation through sowing, to maturity and harvest, so that it was all part of the flow of the garden. It is ironic that much of this carefully orchestrated rhythm plays out unseen and unappreciated because the owners only come here in summer, so miss most of the year's pageant in the garden created specifically for them.

Fernando says that gardens can be art, but not like paintings or sculpture – they are too static for that. For him gardens are more akin to music and his beloved Bach. 'Garden design is to make real abstract and spiritual ideas – however abstract these might be.' I asked if he feels he has to explain these concepts and ideas. 'No, no! Never explain the garden to the client – it has to work for them on their terms. They have to find the concept themselves rather than it being loaded onto them.'

With his reputation of being the most philosophical and intellectual of garden designers, Fernando trusts in the earth and the plants to tell their own story. And it is not all philosophy. Returning to the garden was, he said, a very emotional experience because he gave it birth and now, after 30 years, it has become independent and free.

I asked about the amount of clearly highly tended grass, needing a lot of watering in summer. 'Gardens are an exercise in green with colour fleeting – dancing through the seasons. Green is permanent. The lawns are important in winter – albeit,' he admitted ruefully, 'impractical and very high maintenance in summer.'

I once repeated something that he had said to me in passing at our first meeting, that no garden needed more than eight different plants to be fulfilled, and this was received by the great British

The rich green of the mown grass reaches to the very edge of the cornfield, which is as much part of the garden as the grass or the cypresses and olive trees.

The garden is an essay in the shades and textures of green with, as Caruncho says, just fleeting glimpses of colour.

public with audible gasps of horror. The British culture longs to fill gardens with as many different plants as possible, to load borders and display the range of horticultural acquisitions and the necessary skill in keeping them all happy, but Fernando Caruncho – and I suspect the Spanish soul too – has a fiercer, purer refinement. In this, he is strongly influenced not just by the long Islamic heritage of Andalucía but also Japan. He has completely absorbed the lessons of *ma* and the significance of the space between things, the fullness of the empty space.

I visited the Caruncho studio just outside Madrid, where he has huge scale models of gardens under work laid out. These models are painstakingly accurate down to the last shrub, originally created to show the clients but he told me that working on the scale models is becoming ever more important to the design process. 'The initial sketches are ideas, germs. The models make it real and then the actual making of the garden is an enactment.'

There is an austerity to this, a purity that is perhaps a very Spanish mix of ice and fire. I think of my own way of making a garden, infinitely more clumsy, with days spent moving plants with filthy hands and aching back, feeling my way to some kind of inarticulate balance, almost everything a compromise and rightness almost always more accident than design. Yet there is no living garden designer I admire more.

Torre D'Ariant
MALLORCA

THE ROAD TO TORRE D'ARIANT, UP THE SERRA DE TRAMUNTANA, WHERE THE PYRENEES EMERGE briefly out of the Mediterranean, is long, steep and very winding. A recent storm had left trees scattered and spilt alongside the track and sawdust was still fresh in heaps where the chainsaws cleared the way. Chamaerops palms, fabulously exotic to my northern eye but indigenous to Mallorca, flaunt their ubiquity. Finally, you breast the hills and descend into the bowl of green farmland, the sea stretching north all the way to Barcelona. Down on this north lea of the hills is Torre D'Ariant, the 1,000-hectare (2,500-acre) estate bought by Heidi Gildemeister and her husband, Enrique, in 1980.

Having previously made gardens in Peru and Switzerland, Heidi came to Mallorca expecting to create a lushly planted, sub-tropical garden filled with exotic species, but found that after her first summer most shrivelled up due to lack of water. So she set about creating a garden that could cope with the hot, bone-dry summer conditions and yet be filled with a wide range of plants from all the Mediterranean regions of the world. In 1995, she published the seminal *Mediterranean Gardening: A Waterwise Approach* and she was a founding member of the Mediterranean Garden Society (whose headquarters are the marvellous Garden of Sparoza on the Attica plain outside Athens).

Much of Heidi's book now reads to gardeners entering the second quarter of the twenty-first century as common sense, although 30 years ago, as the impact of climate change was only gradually dawning on the general public, it was radical and the influence of the garden and Heidi's approach has been huge – and increasingly so as the effects of climate change have made their presence felt in gardens all over Europe and not just at its extreme edges.

Certainly, her message was simple. Choose your plants carefully, do not try to grow anything that

does not like hot, dry conditions, put those that need most water nearest the house, let spring and autumn be your prime flowering seasons and learn to accept a summer baking that might reduce some plants to shrivelled brown remnants but – have faith – not kill them.

On the one hand, my own wet, northern garden felt a long way from Heidi's Mediterranean tenets, and on the other, I think I expected something coloured by a conflation of prairie planting and so-called rewilding. But nothing had prepared me for the beauty, scale and richness of Torre D'Ariant. It fits no preconceived notion of the 'correct' way of reacting to climate change – as though there was a moral element involved. This is so much more than a simulacrum of the natural landscape that has been tweaked and monitored to behave within the realms of horticultural decency.

For a start it is brilliantly tended – all four hectares (ten acres) of it by the only full-time gardener Susana Quintanilla – and on top of that it is soaringly beautiful with none of the worthy drabness that shadows many more self-consciously ecologically and environmentally sensitive gardens. There is a richness and variety to the planting, with the plants grouped according to their territories – so those from the Cape are in one section, Australasian ones another, Californians a third and so on. This forms a homogeneity of plants and will be of interest to the botanist but to the visitor walking

Heidi Gildemeister realised that the garden could only be sustainable if it worked with the landscape on its terms rather than to try and follow horticultural convention, and the result is a garden of surpassing beauty.

The house is modest but comfortable and apparently Heidi lived simply, putting all her energy and time into the garden.

along the narrow paths it is all a wonder, these plants from across the world managing to be simultaneously owning the landscape and yet magnificently strange.

The natural rocks and stones of the site are overwhelmingly impressive in themselves, creating drama at every turn, with the backdrop of the mountains behind them. Mature oaks provide shade and structure, and there is a great deal of shaping and pruning and clipping so that the shrubs curve and flow within the rhythm of the rocks in a way that is, of course, highly contrived but absolutely in tune with the landscape it sits in. So we walked through a white area, wooded with a white Judas tree, *Cercis siliquastrum* 'Alba' underplanted with the South African rosemary eriocephalus and the daisy-like flower of felicia sprinkled amongst the stones. Contrived, composed, curated – it feels like a kind of heaven utterly at home on this fierce and stark hillside.

Around the modest farmhouse is a lawn with little red anemones threaded into the coarse grass and clipped cushions of *Pistacia lentiscus*. Collections of aloes and succulents grow in groups. Down a flight of stone steps cut into the rock, a small green pool was reflecting evening light from its backdrop of white stone. The house and garden are domestic spaces, lived in and gardened with simplicity but complete devotion. Fernando Caruncho had told me that Heidi lived a very pure, almost austere life at

Torre D'Ariant, focused almost entirely on the garden. Rather than merely an exercise in creating a garden despite the conditions, it has resulted in a great garden *because* of the conditions.

Heidi Gildemeister's planting is entirely in tune with the local flora – albeit with plants from all over the Mediterranean zones, including Chile, Australasia, South Africa and California, as well as the Mediterranean itself. The management involves using little water but lots of mulch, with every leaf and cut or fallen vegetation composted and recycled. Susana Quintanilla continues this practice assiduously.

However, the genius is not in keeping plants alive in the harshest conditions, but in shaping and clipping and training them in tune with the hills and rocks and great domed crowns of the native trees, so the natural and human world combine to create a garden that is unnatural and contrived – but in harmony with all the elements of its environment and, at every turn, every bend in the hillside path, touching the sublime.

Above: Paths lead from one section to another, each focussing on a particular zone of Mediterranean flora from around the world.

Opposite: The swimming pool is as beautiful as any ornamental water, backed by lovely twists of stone rising out of the water.

Opposite: The Palmeral at Elche is based on systems introduced by the Arabs and thousands of years old. (A moment after this picture was taken, Derry slipped and broke his ankle!)

Overleaf: The Huerto del Cura is a former orchard converted to a garden in the 1940s, with hard paths, bamboos, cacti and pools in amongst the shade of the date palms.

The Palmeral

ELCHE

ELCHE ITSELF IS AN UNREMARKABLE TOWN, DOMINATED IN THE TWENTIETH CENTURY BY ITS SHOE industry, although with a fine ochre stone church, Santa Maria. Should you climb the long, steep, staircase of its bell tower, with its narrow truckle bed in an alcove halfway up for the bell ringer to snooze on, you will be rewarded with a view of the palms spreading out from the flat-roofed centre of town like a rich green ink stain. Elche is worth visiting for its palm trees alone, of which it has the largest concentration in all of Europe and is the most northerly palm grove in the world.

The date palm has had significance in various cultures from being a symbol of fertility to the Egyptians and of victory to the Romans – and it has survived at Elche through Phoenician, Greek, Roman, Carthaginian, Moorish, Visigoth and Christian civilisations. Its greatest threat has come in recent years from its association with Palm Sunday, as five per cent of all the trees were dying each year as a direct result of palm fronds being taken to process through the city, until UNESCO banned this to preserve this World Heritage site.

Elche has had palms, or more specifically, the date palm, *Phoenix dactylifera*, since the fifth century. There are hundreds of thousands of them covering over 500 hectares (1,200 acres), all of which has now been declared a World Heritage site. Date palms were introduced to Spain by Phoenician traders over 2,500 years ago but the current cultivation methods were developed in the eighth century by the Arabs. To this end, they diverted the Vinalopó River so that one half fed the town and the other the date groves. Although some 17 kilometres inland from the Mediterranean shore at Alicante, the Vinalopó is slightly salty, which palms not only tolerate (as do citrus, olives and pomegranates) but actively like.

The traditional eighth-century system of growing the palms is still to be found in Elche. This is based upon small orchards of about one quarter of an acre edged by date palms. These not only

provided the precious dates but shelter for the interior of the orchard where there were two other crops. One was a middle layer of citrus, olive or pomegranate (Elche is still the biggest pomegranate producer in Europe with over 70,000 tons a year), and below that a cereal crop, which would usually be wheat. Around the edge of the orchard was a ditch with high banks where water from the river was directed via sluices and which could be opened out to flood the open ground. As well as providing essential irrigation, this also encouraged the roots of the date palms to spread and anchor the trees better.

Around ten such orchards would be attached to a house amounting to a modern hectare, which was enough to sustain a family and part of a network of hundreds within an area of the Palmeral.

The date harvest is from October to March and only the female trees produce fruit, next year's crop already formed and immature as the current batch is harvested. The males produce a fine yellow pollen that drifts through the network of the orchard boundaries, guaranteed to pollinate as it goes.

Until the 1960s, all the orchards were private, but production dropped and people moved away from the town to nearby countryside to pursue more conventional farming. Many orchards were grubbed up but Elche city council started to buy them and now owns 70 per cent of all the surviving orchards, using them as nurseries for trees to plant in the city. So the centre of each orchard, where previously there would have been fruit underplanted with wheat, is now filled with young street trees ready to be moved to their final urban position.

The Huerto del Cura in the town is a good example of a former orchard being converted to a garden, originally by a priest who grew up there at the end of the nineteenth century – hence the name – and then formally made into a garden in the 1940s, with hard paths, bamboos, cacti and pools in amongst the shade of the date palms.

Below: The irrigation system has remained unchanged for the past two millennia. Water is flooded into the ditches surrounding each orchard which, when damned with sluices, would spill over and flood the open space occupied by a cereal crop and citrus, olive or pomegranate trees. The date palms were grown in squares lining the ditches around each small orchard.

Opposite: The fifteenth-century Torre de los Vaillos in the Palmeral was built as a lookout tower, primarily against the threat of Ottoman invasion from North Africa.

The fourteenth-century Tower of the Infants, plain on the exterior but richly decorated on the inside, looks over a working vegetable garden. The Alhambra was always a series of palaces that needed servicing rather than one coherent building.

The Alhambra
GRANADA

Icons are always difficult to look at, difficult to judge, difficult to know how to approach, and if nothing else, the Alhambra is an icon. It is the best known, most influential and most visited of all Spanish gardens. Fortunately, I have visited a number of times over the years, including three days over 20 years ago when I never left, staying at the Parador within the grounds and able to walk freely alone with my wife after the visitors had left. It was one of the great cultural experiences of my life.

There is no one garden at the Alhambra. It is a loose arrangement of palaces, so it is a collection or succession of gardens, including the oldest Islamic gardens in Europe, amongst the most complete medieval gardens in the world.

Above all, it is the greatest inheritance of Moorish rule in Spain, from the eighth-century Umayyad dynasty to 2 January 1492, when the Alhambra was finally surrendered and the last Sultan of Granada, Boabdil, Abu Abdullah Muhammad XII, rode with his attendants in their full finery to surrender to Ferdinand of Aragon and Isabella of Castile. This was the final day of almost 800 years of Islamic culture that had dominated the Iberian Peninsula. However, the influence in almost every walk of modern Spanish life remains enormously strong and the patio, the enclosed space with water, shade, fragrance, colour and retreat from the heat of the day are still essential elements of all southern Spanish gardens.

The water – brought down from the hillsides beyond Granada, splashing down steps and through channels cut into marble-floored rooms – is a display of wealth and power to match any precious metal. The timing of the buildings – from the middle of the thirteenth century to the middle of the fourteenth – coincides with the development of irrigation. This is an expression of the way that water, as much as stone, wood and plaster, can be harnessed for pleasure.

The first fortified buildings on the site of the Alhambra were built in the middle of the thirteenth century by al-Ahmar, the first Nasrid king. His grandson, Ismail I, added much at the beginning of the fourteenth century and the greatest period of building was during the rule of Emir Muhammad V, in the second half of the fourteenth century.

These stages involved remodelling existing buildings and butting new palaces up against them in what seems an arbitrary and almost random accretion, including Charles V's palace building crassly slammed down in the centre that was never finished, never lived in and roofless for over 400 years.

The site adjusted as it went, meaning that there is now no grand procession or route through. Your journey is more akin to wandering into back streets from magnificent buildings and then out again via a small side door into another palatial space, slipping from century to century from the palaces of the Mexuar, Comares, Court of the Lions and the Partal Gardens.

To understand the Alhambra, you have to set everything into the context of the Islamic faith and the notion of paradise as a garden. The exterior of the Alhambra is plain to the point of functional austerity but the interior of the buildings and the gardens that they are wrapped around are embellished and decorated to jewel-like intensity.

The sense of gardens being hidden within buildings would have been much greater in the Alhambra's fourteenth- and fifteenth-century heyday because many buildings have disappeared from what was effectively a small city, and their presence is now marked by gardens, the walls becoming hedges, corridors or paths, and rooms patios or borders. This tends to give the modern Alhambra a false sense of shared, public gardens that the tourists, by their hundreds of thousands, wander through. But originally the gardens were places of private pleasure and as intimately connected to the buildings and their occupants as any of the rooms.

However, this intimacy and privacy did not mean that some were not – and remain – breathtakingly grand, even monumental. Thus, the Patio de Comares is starkly simple with its long block of black water edged by thick myrtle hedges but somehow – overwhelmingly – beautiful and satisfying.

The Court of the Lions, constructed in the second half of the fourteenth century by Sultan Mohammed V, now an expanse of marble, was originally a conventional *charbagh*, the four quarters sunken beds filled with plants, somewhat like the Patio de las Doncellas in the Real Alcázar in Seville, surrounded by the slim columns representing palm trees in an oasis, watered from the central fountain and all hidden and accessible only to the royal family.

The Partal Palace does not have the grandeur of the Nasrid Palace surrounding at the Court of the Lions, but the garden is the most accessible of the complex. The building sits before a large square pool fed from a series of higher tanks and rills, running sweetly through mosaicked cobbled paths, down the centre of steps into channels and on to the building. There is a purity, a refinement about it that is unimprovable.

Across a narrow valley is the Generalife, originally the sultan's hunting lodge before passing into private ownership in 1429, where it remained, in the same family, until the 1920s. The slopes are still covered with vegetables and fruits grown for the palaces, and now the gardens include an outdoor theatre space, but the Generalife, like the rest of the complex, was once very private, a retreat from

An early morning view across to the main set of buildings from the Generalife, showing how the Alhambra is like a small hilltop town.

the summer heat of the busy streets and thousands of people that occupied the Alhambra. (Although it can be very cold too. I have been there in February where it barely rose above freezing for days and all water in fountains, rills, jets and pools remained frozen solid.)

The Generalife garden stretches to 12 hectares (30 acres) of cypress walks, rose gardens and endless ornately pebbled paths weaving through the shade. But the patio with its central canal, arcing jets and bright carpet planting in the sunken beds, all carefully restored in the 1930s, is the most famous part of both it and the Alhambra in its entirety.

There is debate over whether the famous avenue of waterspouts along the central canal in the garden court of the Generalife is an original Moorish feature because it has been suggested that this is too noisy and dramatic for Islamic tastes and is thus almost a Disneyfication of the idea of a paradise garden. It is somewhat reminiscent of the baroque eighteenth-century water sprays in the Alfabia Garden. But it is too late to stop this being one of the most iconic water features of any kind anywhere in the world.

I do not know if it will ever again be possible to visit the Alhambra alone, as my wife and I did in winter 2004, the place entirely to ourselves for hours on end, but even jostled by crowds and with all the frustrations of any huge tourist destination, it remains one of the great gardens of the world.

Opposite: The avenue of water jets running along the central canal in the Patio de la Acequias of the Generalife is one of the most iconic images in the world. The sunken beds on either side are filled with flowers and the Generalife with its enclosed, cool fountains and flowers was a place for the Sultan to retreat to in the heat of summer.

Below: In keeping with Islamic building traditions, the exteriors of the various buildings in the Alhambra are plain and simple but the interiors are exquisitely decorated with Nasrid plasterwork, often of dazzling intricacy.

Below: The gardens of the Partal Palace both reflect the gardens that were originally part of the Islamic palace and were created on the footprint of former buildings.

Opposite: The Jardines Bajos or Lower Gardens were added in the 1920s and 1930s after the State acquired the Generalife, and were designed in Islamic style as the public approach to the palace.

The garden has a large collection of palms and cycads, contributing to the intensely rich vegetation set in the surrounding harsh Andalusian landscape.

The Botanic Garden Málaga
Jardín Botánico Histórico La Concepción
MÁLAGA

JORGE LORING Y OYARZÁBAL WAS THE SPANISH NAME OF THE MARQUÉS DE CASA LORING BUT he was also known as George Henry Loring to his American family, and the combination of the two cultures shaped his life and his garden.

His father was an American who moved to Málaga and married a local woman. Jorge/George, born in 1822, was one of their sons. He was educated at Harvard before returning to Spain and Málaga, bringing with him a nineteenth-century American energy to his commercial and political life, building the first railroad in Andalucía from Córdoba to Málaga, founding the Bank of Málaga, amassing a collection of antiquities that in 2016 became the Museo de Málaga and starting the newspaper *El Correo de Andalucía*. He was also an MP and senator in Madrid. The marquisate was created for him in 1856 as a result of his charitable work during an outbreak of cholera in Málaga. So all in all, a good and highly successful egg.

The Jardín Botánico Histórico La Concepción is on the northern edge of the city, set up on the hillside looking over the looping highways, factories and urban sprawl of what is now the sixth biggest city in Spain with over half a million inhabitants. It is not a beautiful view but little of that would have been here when the family farm of the Marqués and Marquesa de Casa Loring was developed by them into a substantial house in 1855. Amalia and Jorge immediately set to planting the grounds with specimens collected from all over the world, creating their own private, but extensive, botanic garden, which came to be called 'La Concepción' after one of their daughters.

This is gardening on the grandest of scales, extending to 25 hectares (61 acres), and was the result of their honeymoon travels taking them to a number of great gardens around Europe, inspiring them to create their own version, but with the same energy and ambition that built railroads and founded newspapers. As they lived mainly in Madrid, as all grand families did and still do, it was a hobby, a private passion, along with the love of archaeology that ultimately resulted in the modern Museo de Málaga. It was a joint work, with Amalia mostly in charge of the garden. She hired a French gardener, Jacinto Chamoussent, to run the project, scouring nurseries all over Europe for plants.

I was taken up through the steep winding paths – intended to be strolled – in a dramatic buggy ride overhung with trees, creepers, palms, bamboos and a richness of vegetation that is surreally at variance with the Andalusian baked landscape beyond. We passed by and under a huge Moreton Bay fig, *Ficus macrophylla*, casuarinas, Norfolk Island pines and magnolias fat with flower. In the undergrowth, clivias, monstera and glimpses of strelitzias and cycads loom and flash by as we head uphill. There are over 2,000 species of sub-tropical plants here in what is the only sub-tropical botanical garden in Europe.

Breaking out into the open amongst a grove of superb plane trees, there is substantial development of new beds for succulents edged with drystone walls overhung with great banks of prostrate rosemary and broad paths. This is all the work of the city council, which has owned La Concepción since 1990. But follow these newly gravelled paths and freshly planted beds and you come to the Mirador, built just after the First World War. By then, the Loring offspring had sold the estate to the Echevaría Azcarate family from the Basque Country. They continued collecting and planting and expanding the garden's reach, as well as building the Mirador and the long pool behind it.

The Mirador, with its tiled cupola sitting on eight pillars hybridising Islamic and bandstand architecture, was sited to look out over the empty countryside to Málaga and the sea beyond – and there are photographs of the family posing by the new building with just that scenery behind them. But now there is a tangle of motorways whose roar is constant, factories, houses splashed out onto open hillsides, cranes, the top of a huge cruise ship, with the sea a vague smear below the horizon. So much for the view. Better to turn and look back at the garden.

Málaga was a Republican stronghold during the Civil War but when Franco's forces took the city the house was run as a training school for officers and subsequently as a political training base for the right-wing Falange and much of the estate was confiscated. However, the garden was declared a site of Historical and Artistic Interest.

The garden remained in hands of the Echevaría family – who founded Iberia airlines – until 1990, falling increasingly into neglect and disrepair from the mid-1960s. The city's purchase was a rescue operation and they have created a number of new areas as well as the extensive succulent beds and classified and arranged the planting more systematically. The result, despite the spoilt view from the Mirador, is a fascinating collection, immaculately maintained and displayed.

The Mirador was built in 1920 to survey the then almost empty view out across the countryside to the sea beyond. It now looks over motorways, industrial sites and thousands of residential buildings all but obscuring the sea.

Opposite: The trunk and roots of a huge Moreton Bay fig create sculptural, flanged buttresses.

Below: A wisteria, recently hard-pruned, becomes an extension of the railings on an outdoor stair.

Opposite: The front courtyard of the house is designed as a space for parties with shade provided by citrus trees, the linearity of the building softened by drifts and hedges of rosemary.

Overleaf: The designer Fernando Martos has used a matrix of the grass pennisetum 'Fairy Tale' through which are planted gaura, salvias, pomegranate trees and unclipped mounds of myrtle.

The Guadalmina Garden
MARBELLA

MARBELLA IS A STRANGE PLACE. IT HAS CHARMING BACK STREETS AND THE STUNNING PARQUE de la Alameda in the centre of the old town, like an outdoor version of the Atocha station in Madrid, with its palms, bananas, ficus and green over-arching opulence. But Marbella and that particular stretch of coast has long attracted money and the flaunting of wealth. We went to visit a garden in Guadalmina Baja that was beautiful, inspiring and yet only made because someone with a very great deal of money was prepared to hand creative freedom to a young designer they respected and admired.

The Guadalmina area is largely occupied by an exclusive housing estate whose high gates and walls hide all but a screen of trees and hedges from its roads. There are, inevitably, golf courses. It is the other side of the Puerto Banús coin, the careful anonymity of the wealthy banker and lawyer rather than the flashy display of the international wide boy.

But once inside, past the gatekeeper and guard, the garden behind these particular vast solid metal gates is a delight. The designer Fernando Martos and his wife, Clara, were waiting to show me round. Fernando studied in Madrid but then worked as a gardener at Newby Hall in Yorkshire and with Tom Stuart-Smith on a garden in Mallorca. He visits English gardens regularly and is clearly influenced by a British style of planting.

When the current owner bought the 1.2-hectare (three-acre) plot in 2018, there was already an established house and garden complete with swimming pool, but he bulldozed the lot and, during the course of the pandemic, built a brand new house with guest and staff houses, new swimming pool and tennis court. This done, he gave Fernando free rein to create a garden to complement the architecture.

The garden was less than two years old when I visited in spring of 2023 but already managed to walk the line between satisfying the need for instant gratification that extreme wealth demands, with the necessary stages of gradual becoming that every good garden has to go through.

In front of the house, behind a wall that keeps parked cars out of sight, is a gravelled forecourt the same sandy colour as the sleek fortress walls of the house, with its enormous expanses of darkened plate glass, a long pond and standard citrus. This is a space, like the one at Dehesa de Yonte near Ávila, for parties and gatherings, cooly stylish but also rather formal. Go round the corner of the building and this changes completely.

Although he was quick to explain that the climate of Marbella needs an entirely different palette of plants, Fernando admitted that he is trying to create a Mediterranean version of Newby Hall in this large area to one side of the building that revolves around a huge – and apparently very productive – avocado tree. It is a largely un-Spanish sensitivity to colour and flower, coupled with a Mediterranean use of shade and structure. It is a strikingly successful combination.

Cloud hedges of myrtle and box bound large borders filled with flowering perennials – lots of salvias, dahlias, leonotis, agapanthus and perovskia in blues, oranges and purple. The planting is still young enough to show a lot of mulched ground lined with irrigation pipes. Fernando told me that the supply of water was not a problem, as plenty comes down from the mountains. As well as the large avocado, there is a giant jelly palm, *Butia capita*, both of which had survived the bulldozer – although the latter adds a level of incongruity to the Newby Hall-by-Marbella vibe.

Round the corner again, via a long-flagged metal pergola waiting to be covered by the wisteria that was valiantly edging up the sides, and the tone and planting palette changes completely. A grid of paths reflecting the severe horizontal lines of the building form a series of huge square beds that are planted simply in the prairie style, based upon a matrix of the grass pennisetum 'Fairy Tale', that repeats and flows through the beds, lots of gaura, unclipped myrtle and pomegranate trees spaced out amongst, and rising from, the low underplanting.

Large but newly planted cork oaks flank the broad path leading down to a pool complex with seemingly a dozen or more settees beneath an elaborate metal framework around it, as yet unclothed by the climbers planted to provide shade. Tall palms reflect in the turquoise water and obscure the neighbours which, for all the obvious luxury, are set cheek by jowl in every direction.

Below the pool is a large immaculate lawn, out of sight of the house, so not in itself the obvious trophy that large immaculate lawns are by definition in the Marbella climate, but apparently intended as a setting for parties. A professionally set-up tennis court is accompanied by cooly glaucous planting, dominated by huge melianthus, to screen its netting. There are variations of this all over the region, with houses kitted out with all the conventional facilities for a modern, luxury holiday in the sun – but vanishingly few also have the rare luxury of a fine garden. I asked Fernando what visitors to the house made of his garden, wondering if it was as appreciated as it should be. They are surprised, he said, because it is not common to have such a big area of only plants. But Fernando's 'only plants' has created a garden that is uncommonly good by any standards, in any setting, and how admirable of the owner to be a patron of this truly superb garden by a young and brilliant designer.

Clipped mounds of teucrium create sculptural structure alongside a shady walk in the lower part of the garden.

The allotments were created as an opportunity for local residents to grow their own fresh, organic produce. There is no waiting list, no fee, no need to own tools or have previous experience – just the willingness to grow.

The Marbella Arboretum Allotments

MARBELLA

On the northern edge of Marbella, backing on to rough scrub and farmland, is a small group of allotments on the site of what was a municipal rubbish dump. At first glance this is admirable but ordinary, another allotment site of hundreds of thousands around the world. But the story of the Marbella arboretum is inspiring and uplifting and the measure of human happiness created here spreads far beyond its seemingly everyday credentials.

It began with the need of an Argentinian, Alejandro Orioli, to repay what he felt was a debt to Spain for taking him in 30 years ago and giving him a good life. He told me that he thought long and hard about how to make the biggest impact and came to the conclusion that, now in the twenty-first century, empowering people to do practical things was the most beneficial thing he could do. So he would provide the opportunity, tools and skills for local people to grow good food, consequentially equipping them to teach and encourage others in turn.

He found this site and organised and financed the clearing away of 60 large lorry loads of rubbish before they could begin. He built sheds, brought in topsoil, made raised beds and paths, and then they were ready to begin. And this was just the beginning, because unlike at any other allotment site I have visited, Alejandro and his son Ivo provide much more than just a growing space. All anyone has to do is to live locally and turn up. As well as a plot, averaging 40 square metres, Alejandro and Ivo will provide seeds – all of which are raised by Ivo on site – tools and instruction.

On a Sunday morning the place was busy. The activities were all familiar but the palette of plants was different to anything in the UK – certainly at the end of April. People, mostly middle-aged and mostly in straw hats, were staking metre-high tomatoes, tying in supports for peppers and aubergines, drawing up the soil for small, temporary raised beds. There was lots of fennel and onions, cabbages and chard allowed to go to seed for collection. It was already too hot for lettuces to be at all happy so they were noticeable by their scarcity compared to any British allotment.

Alejandro has no formal horticultural qualifications but Ivo trained at the University of Huelva and at Dartington College in England, and acts as a kind of resident horticultural reference library for the allotmenteers and the source of most of its seeds. He showed me his own area that was devoted entirely to the production of seeds. He told me that he had 131 different varieties of seed to distribute around the allotment holders. There was an element of closed shop about this, because one of the conditions of using the allotment was that no one was allowed to bring in any seed without specific dispensation from him to certify them as organic. Excess seeds, produce and eggs from the chickens are sold to put money back into the site.

A table and chairs were set beneath the branches of a mulberry- and jasmine-festooned bothy where people could sit in the shade and admire their work. It is a small thing but the difference that consistently dry weather makes to the day-to-day business of cultivation is huge. So much of British allotment life is founded in mud.

We had a simple but delicious lunch in the shade of a tree with bread made by Alejandro, homemade cheese, his honey and *pan con tomate*. It all amounted to the hippy dream made hard-edged enough to sustain and fit seamlessly into ordinary muddled lives – based upon Alejandro and Ivo's desire to give back to the community that embraced them.

That is how it was when I left in April 2023, filled with admiration for what they had achieved and how it might develop in the future. Subsequently, I heard that the site had been vandalised and that Alejandro and Ivo were no longer associated with it. The dream was over – or at least had moved on.

Below: The allotments are on the site of an old dump and over 60 lorry loads of rubbish had to be taken away before ground work could begin.

Opposite: Each plot is about 40 square metres, all tools can be provided and all the seeds are grown organically on site.

The town has been transformed by a decision to add flowers and plants of all kinds to every street and corner, with the tradition of pots attached to the walls of houses and patios to the fore.

Estepona
COSTA DEL SOL

Carry on west down the A7 that splits the upmarket Guadalmina district and you enter the municipality of Estepona and, 20 kilometres further on, the town of the same name. Estepona is bright and very sunny and famous for its beaches. This was fine for tourists but there was a major logistical problem for locals.

Until recently, the main road ran along the seafront and you risked life and limb crossing it anywhere other than at designated points. As well as this being tedious and making pedestrians subservient to the car, it was noisy, smelly, polluting and set a drab, car-dominated tone. But the city has tackled this with dramatic results – and its main weapon has been flowers.

Where the road once ran along Avenida de España is now pedestrianised and children, people walking their dogs, joggers, rollerbladers and cyclists all easily mingle and amble gently where the traffic formerly roared. Where white lines ran down the middle of the road is now a garden, a kilometre long with islands of trees and beds rich with colour.

Colour is the key to this transformation. Where 'going green' and 'greening the city' have become catchphrases, Estepona uses green only as a backdrop to the bright primary colours of flowers in painted pots. The council does all the growing, raising over a million flowers and trees in their own nurseries and undertaking all the planting and maintenance so that local people have no responsibility of care but every opportunity for enjoyment.

Although local people do not have to maintain the plants, every neighbourhood is involved from the outset in what is growing in their street. So they get together and choose the colour of the pots hanging from the walls with every street identified by its own colour, and they also get a choice of the plants that they like. In other words, the scheme has not been foisted onto people because they

Opposite: Each street selects its preferred colour for the pots that adorn it, providing a unity of design.

Right: Trees, flower beds and water features have replaced random on-street parking across the town, retaining access for cars but hugely improving the quality of urban life for pedestrians and residents.

ought to like it but they have bought into it very the earliest stages. It is also, of course, reminiscent of the Moorish patios and use of pots that you find in private houses all across Andalucía.

All the pots – and there are over 16,000 of them – are hand watered, twice a week. Whilst this might seem unnecessarily labour intensive, I remember interviewing a gardener on his roof garden who said he eschewed an irrigation system because hand watering was his main active relationship with the plants – it was the sum of his gardening. I can see that the council team coming round twice a week to water, to show that the plants are being cared for and nurtured, is reassuring and part of the active involvement that makes the planting more than just decoration.

And there is much more than just thousands of brightly painted pots. Streets have been reshaped and designed to accommodate water features, parking lots moved and made into gardens and even houses bought and pulled down to be replaced with gardens. In all, 135 streets have been renovated and 14 kilometres of roads moved or restored to pedestrians.

The involvement of locals has a very human touch too. A row of trees in full pink flower had little hand-painted dedications and names at their base. It turns out that when a child is born the parents can contact the council and adopt a tree for that child for the rest of its life. I asked how much that cost? Nothing. It is, I was told, a spiritual connection and thus beyond and perhaps above any price.

The whole project is not without problems – in early spring of 2023, they had very bad salt winds that burnt and killed many plants and they say that this seems to be getting worse with climate change. But the programme is budgeted to extend further over the coming years and the town is committed to it, not least because the quality of life for all is so obviously improved.

Casa del Rey Moro

RONDA

THE ROAD FROM MARBELLA TO RONDA WINDS ITS WAY TORTUOUSLY THROUGH THE HILLS OF Parque Nacional de la Sierra de las Nieves. It took us to our lodgings for the night in a hotel down a long track that gave every appearance of being a ranch but whose decor was a marriage of Liberace and Louis XIV with a sprinkling of Dalí for good measure. Refreshed, albeit slightly startled, we headed into Ronda early in the morning to visit the Casa del Rey Moro.

Its story is a good, if somewhat complicated, one.

The name Ronda comes from the Moorish Izn-Rand-Onda or 'City of the Castle' and it was one of the last Moorish strongholds to fall to the Christians in 1485. In 1570, under the orders of Philip II, all remaining Moors were expelled from the city. This means that, despite the romanticism of the association, Casa del Moro, which was not built for another 200 years, has no Moorish connection at all.

No matter. A little historical leeway with the facts can be forgiven as embellishment rather than deception. The house is situated dramatically on the very edge of the 100-metre-deep canyon of the Guadalevín River that splits the town and which made it so easy to defend. There are steps down the side of this ravine that date from the fourteenth century, when the Moors carved a fortress into the cliffs below the modern house with access to the river and thus water.

The horticultural history of the garden begins in the twentieth century, when the house was bought by Duquesa de Parcent in 1910 as a retreat from her main house in Madrid. In 1912, she hired the eminent French designer Jean Claude Forestier – who, as well as many public commissions in his native Paris, Buenos Aires and Lisbon, designed the Parque de María Luisa in Seville and the garden in the Plaça de Joan Fiveller as part of the Parc de la Ciutadella in Barcelona – to create a garden for her. To that end, she also bought up neighbouring houses and pulled them down to make the site for the garden bigger.

Nevertheless, despite this architectural razing, the site is awkward, being long and narrow, dropping 100 metres to the river below on one side and bounded by a street on the other and Forestier's training as an engineer as well as a designer was needed to create links between the three levels. He drew upon the Moorish traditions of Ronda and created a garden using Islamic styles and idioms, such as the central fountain (brought by the duquesa from Paris), a rill running down paved steps, locally made, richly glazed tiles in blues, terracotta and white, also all made in Ronda, symmetry defined by myrtle hedges and the use of fragrance from rosemary, myrtle, thyme and jasmine. This fusion of Spanish, Islamic and, to a certain extent, French influences was a new style that came to be known as 'neo-Arabic'.

On one side is the ravine with all its plunging drama, and the other, behind a wall, a street, hidden but heard. But the end of the garden has a long view stretching out across the Andalusian landscape of vineyards, olive groves, and citrus and pomegranate orchards. A peacock struts along the tiled parapet above the gorge, its iridescent feathers matching the blue and green glazing, its tail sweeping the floor as it stands possessively on the wall and then, head back, calls out and shuffles its raised tail like a deck of gorgeous cards.

Early photographs of the garden show the palms, cedars and cypresses that Forestier planted as small, and the garden consequently more open, but a century later, they have outgrown the garden. However, their scale provides blessed shade, and, as always with a smallish space, actually makes it seem bigger.

The garden is now beautifully kept, hedges clipped tight, not a weed despoiling the raked soil between the roses in the small parterres. But the ownership is the subject of some dispute.

The duquesa died in 1937 and the property passed through a number of owners before ending up in the hands of an octogenarian gypsy woman. At the end of the 1990s a German property developer, Jochen Knie, living in Seville, visited the house and, according to him, agreed to buy the house, wrote a cheque there and then and received a receipt written on a napkin.

Jochen took possession and started on repairs and renewals. But the Spanish government had declared it a national monument, which made the transaction invalid. Jochen was evasive about the current ownership but I met him in the garden and he still seemed proprietorial, though he does not live there and was unwilling to talk in anything but the vaguest terms.

However, regardless of ownership, the garden is open and can, and should, be visited as a minor but fascinating gem.

Opposite: The central fountain was originally installed in the conservatory of the duquesa's Paris home before being brought to the garden, but was later stolen. However, it was rediscovered and returned to the garden in 2019.

Overleaf: The garden culminates in a wellhead. Early photographs show the garden as open with broad views to the countryside outside Ronda but Forestier's trees have now been allowed to grow huge, providing shade at the expense of visibility.

Below: The garden sits like a balcony above the cliff face of the gorge, giving it stupendous views across the old town and countryside beyond.

Opposite: Forestier designed the garden around a rill that takes water from the highest pont of the garden down its length via a series of pools and fountains, as a conscious nod to the long Islamic heritage of Ronda and Andalucía.

The Patio de las Doncellas, or 'Court of the Maidens', was paved over until 2007 when it was restored to reveal this superb example of an Islamic paradise garden with its sunken beds and central canal set in the glorious Mudejar decorative architecture.

Real Alcázar
SEVILLE

On an early spring morning take the gate into the former stable yard of the Real Alcázar, and you will enter an open area of beaten earth surrounded by a double square of citrus trees in full blossom, from which comes a heady cloud of fragrance. Before you even buy a ticket this is the most richly sensuous entry I have made into any garden in the world.

The entrance to the Real Alcázar in Seville is in the shadow of Seville Cathedral's Giralda tower, built originally as the minaret but which now houses the 24 bells that ring the hour. This conflation of Moorish and Christian meets its apogee in the Alcázar. There was an Islamic fortress on the site dating from the tenth century, and it is the oldest continuously occupied royal palace in Europe. Like the Alhambra, it is a collection of palaces, with their own gardens, rather than one integral building. But unlike the Alhambra which in its vastness feels like a small city, with thousands of attendants and craftsmen servicing the court, the Alcázar, for all its regal grandeur, has an intimacy. It feels enclosed and its splendour is secret and exclusive.

The intimate Islamic gardens that were made without any desire or need for vistas, avenues or carefully contrived glimpses of gardens beyond, evolved into spaces designed for Christian courtiers to parade, and yet still with the very Islamic myrtle hedges and essential fruits of dates, figs, pomegranates and oranges.

Whereas the water in the Islamic period would have been constrained and contained in rills and bubbling fountains, it is now channelled in a grander and very un-Islamic ostentatious fashion with the Estanque de Mercurio, that was once a Moorish reservoir backed by the palace wall, now fed by a stream of water jetting dramatically from the roof. However, it is this melding of the two radically different styles that is so particular to Andalucía in general and the Real Alcázar in particular.

At the heart of the palace is the Patio de las Doncellas, or 'Court of the Maidens', built in high Mudejar style. Like the Court of the Lions in the Alhambra, this was paved over with marble slabs under the reign of Philip II in the 1580s, but in 2007 it was restored to its original layout with deeply sunken beds, flanking a long basin lined in blue tiles. The foliage, flowers and fruit of the orange trees in the beds are consequently at head height as you walk between them and the basin, the fragrance deliberately inches from your nose and the fruits within easy plucking reach. The ground beneath the citrus is planted with bulbs and annual flowers to create a floral carpet in spring. This is a pure paradise garden, filled with water, flowers, fruit, birdsong and shade, surrounded with exquisite plasterwork and tiles – all made by local Moorish artisans in the 1360s for the Spanish Christian king, Pedro I.

Pedro is known to history as Pedro the Cruel, which was probably apt given the accounts of various appalling deeds he instigated, but perhaps all of a piece in a particularly turbulent and cruel period of European history. However, in building his central palace he never sought to suppress or

Above: The combination of Islamic features such as the pool and fountain with the very Western gateway and railings beyond leading to the eighteenth-century gardens is a reflection of the way the two cultures have remained bound in Andalucía.

Opposite: The intermingling of two cultures can be seen in the classical columns coupled with intensive use of Islamic tiles in the foreground and 'Seville' oranges in the background – only bitter oranges were known during the Islamic period, with the first record of sweet oranges in Europe being in the 1470s.

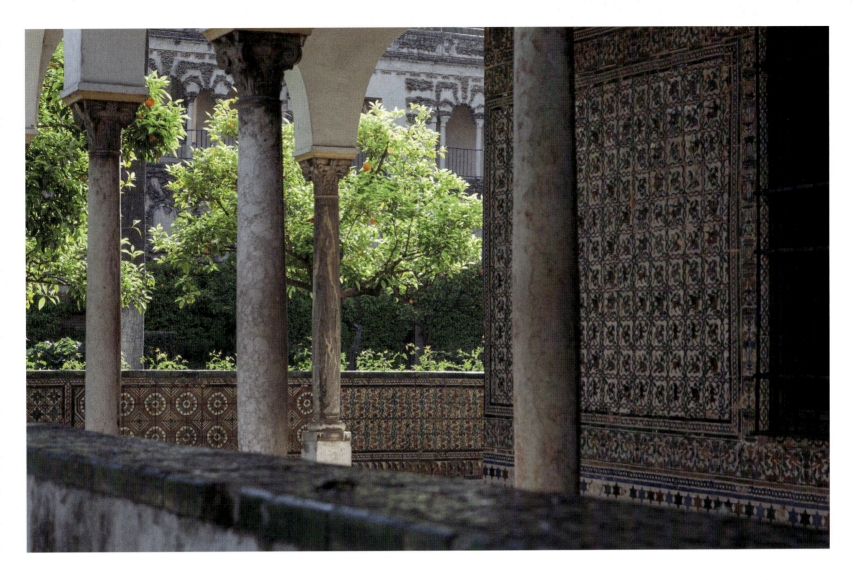

Overleaf: The main water feature, the Estanque de Mercurio, is fed by a stream of water jetting dramatically from the roof and the old wall backing it is made into a loggia embellished and encrusted like a grotto.

obliterate the nearly 600 years of Islamic rule, which had lasted until Fernando III of Castile conquered the region in 1248. Pedro's building in the complex is one of the best examples of the Mudejar, where Christian and Islamic style come home comfortably together. Most of the craftsmen were Muslims and there is evidence that Emir Muhammad V at the Alhambra was influenced by its construction so there was a cross-fertilisation that ran in both directions.

As a result of his support for the Sultan of Granada, Pedro was given a huge ruby and this whopping great stone now sits at the centre of the British Imperial State Crown, having been passed on by Pedro to the Black Prince, eldest son of Edward III, for his assistance during the Hundred Years' War.

In the sixteenth century, as silver and gold began to come in from the New World – all arriving here in Seville – the new wealth transformed the intimate, enclosed Moorish gardens into ever grander and more expansive grounds, parterres and walks. The Moorish orchards became Italianate gardens and this process continued into the seventeenth century under Philip III, when the Muslim wall behind the

Estanque de Mercurio was transformed into the current ornate loggia. This is embellished and encrusted like a Renaissance grotto, looking into the palace interior across the water on one side and out into the Jardín del Marqués de la Vega Inclán with its palms and neatly clipped parterres on the other. This latter was created in 1913, strongly influenced by Jean Claude Forestier's Parque de María Luisa, the Moorish influence visibly diluting, the gardens becoming more of an international hybrid as you move further away from the palace buildings – in distance and in time – with a maze and 'English' gardens.

But it is back in the core of the palace, interweaving and conjoining in a series of barely connecting buildings, creating spaces for the intimate oases surviving from the Islamic period and, best of all, Pedro's Mudejar integration of the best of Islamic craftsmanship in the Patio de las Doncellas, that is the real glory of the Alcázar.

Below and opposite: The Jardín del Marqués de la Vega Inclán was made between 1913 and 1917, using a grid of walkways and hedges with rills and fountains as a cool, very formal woodland.

The Jardín Grande at Casa de Pilatos was made on the site of an orchard in the final years of the sixteenth century and was strongly influenced by Italian Renaissance gardens.

Casa de Pilatos
SEVILLE

As with so many gardens in southern Europe, the key to the garden at Casa de Pilatos is water. The house was built in the 1480s around its own supply of water from the Roman aqueduct. This was exceptional because nearly all water supplies at the time were property of the crown. To have your own dedicated supply of water for drinking, cooking, bathing and irrigation was a rare privilege.

The house is owned and run by the Casa Ducal de Medinaceli Foundation, who also own Pazo de Oca in Galicia (page 21), which the Medinaceli family use as a summer residence. The original owner of the site and builder of the house was a member of the powerful Ribera family. His son, the first Marqués de Tarifa, made a pilgrimage to Jerusalem and Italy in 1520 and from that trip came, somewhat convolutedly and much later in the eighteenth century, the name 'Casa de Pilatos' which referred to Pontius Pilate's house in Jerusalem, as well as much of the Renaissance influence in the building that came as a direct result of the Italian part of his Grand Tour.

The first patio is dominated by its central marble fountain brought to the house from Genoa in 1529. It sets the tone and the overall impression is one of somewhat austere Renaissance grandeur. This is reinforced by the large classical sculptures in each corner, magnificent but slightly at odds with the Mudejar decoration, the slender columns and ornate glazed tiles of the walls under the cloistered colonnade. The patio is paved with black and white marble radiating out from the central fountain in a pattern cruder but more authoritative and dominant than the more subtle intricacies of the Moorish embellishment it combines with. In short, it absorbs both its Islamic and Christian heritage into an incredibly impressive statement of power.

There is a domestic element to this too. Until the 1980s, this was the private home of the Dukes of Segorbe. I was told by Sol (María de la Blanca de Medina y Orléans-Braganza), Countess of Ampurias,

whose grandmother started the Casa Ducal de Medinaceli Foundation in 1980, and who, amongst a long armful of other titles, will inherent the Dukedom of Segorbe from her father, the touchingly ungrand aside that when she was a child this palatial courtyard was an ideal place to rollerblade in the evenings after it was closed to the public.

Walk right, through the beautifully rich Salón del Pretorio, and you come to the Jardín Chico, with a rectangular basin lined with pelargoniums in pots shoulder to terracotta shoulder around its edge, which is where the original water supply came in from the Roman aqueduct. I had visited in February when the bones were not fleshed with flower, but in April the roses spilled freely and the green of the myrtle, box and bay still glowed with spring freshness.

The Salón Dorado, with its gold ceiling and walls painted the *albero* ochre of the sandy paths outside, adorned with classical bas-reliefs and sections and fragments of classical sculptures, has three external walls pierced by grille, glassless windows, the better to sit in the cool shade and enjoy the garden.

A basin lined with terracotta pots in the Jardín Chico is fed by the original fifteenth-century water supply. The houses crowded around the edge of the garden are a reminder that this is in the heart of the city.

To one side of the Salón Dorado is a garden filled with gold and purple planting, dominated by palms and the standard rose 'Carte d'Or'.

To one side is a small garden filled with 'Carte d'Or' standard roses and palms exactly the colour of the beaten sand paths around a six-sided pool. It is backed by a high wall of clipped star jasmine and steps on the other side lead up under a huge *Magnolia grandiflora* to the raised garden filled with soft pink roses. It is both sun-filled and fresh on a day when the heat is thickening the air before the morning has really begun.

Plumbago, wisteria and ivy smother the enclosing walls, creating a scale that is domestic and surprisingly intimate. Walking through the garden is like being in a large open-plan room with different functions in different parts of the space, but seen through the barred windows of the Salón Dorado, the garden is a series of tableaux, each complete unto itself, each with the accompaniment of that precious water gently splashing.

Across the other side of the main courtyard is the Jardín Grande. This had been the orchard or *huerta* for the household until the end of the sixteenth century, when the Italian architect Benvenuto Tortello was hired to create a garden in the Italian style, complete with parterre, sculptures and trees, a

Left: The beaten sand paths exactly replicate the *albero* colour of the walls, intensifying the golden colour of this corner of the garden.

Opposite: Clipped citrus trees provide rhythm, structure and shade in the Jardín Grande.

large fountain in the centre and two large loggias added at either end with a third on the north side.

The garden lives up to its name. It is distinctly big and grand and a bravura display of Renaissance design. The citrus trees are clipped at just above eye height, so creating a green umbrella against the sun, shading the bright pink 'Knock Out' rose from America that fills each of the myrtle-hedged beds of the parterre and picks up the lurid shout of colour from the bougainvillea on the walls, somehow settling and steadying both into an acceptable balanced level that does not disrupt the intended harmony – and a kind of palatial harmonious intimacy is exactly what is achieved.

The ground-level loggia and the two first-floor ones at either end are big enough to contain an invited crowd but small enough to encourage dalliance. The rhythm of the mushroom citrus and the bay lollipops within the high pink crenellated walls has the visual effect of gently running water. It soothes and slows. The only jarring and rather unexpected note comes from the inclusion of pillars of clipped Irish yew – evidently unhappy in the Seville heat and visibly fading.

It is a garden for assignments and intrigue, grand and yet hidden by high walls, and all the more exclusive and remarkable for being completely surrounded by the narrow streets of the old city.

Left: A grilled window in the Salón Dorado frames a date palm and smaller – but probably older – sago palm.

Opposite: The first patio is paved in marble and is a combination of intricate Mudejar plasterwork and classical sculptures collected from Renaissance Italy.

Overleaf: The Jardín Grande has a loggia at either end and this on one side providing beautifully proportioned spaces for both entertainment and quiet enjoyment of the garden.

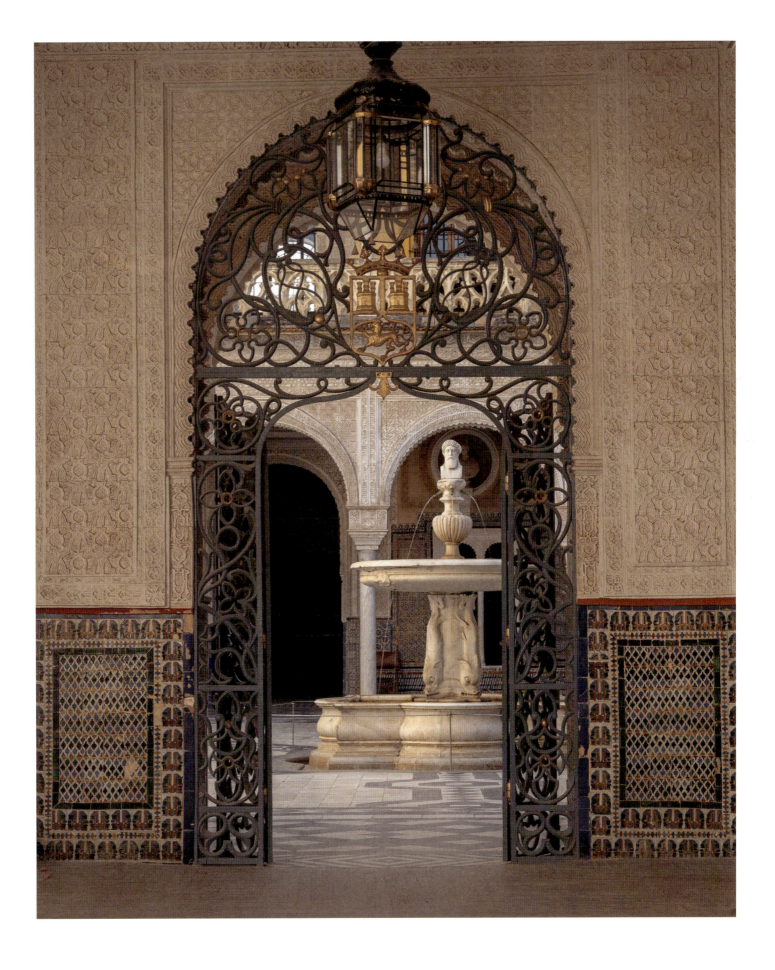

Palms rise in the first patio to the roof and above, bringing the garden up into the first floor rooms and the arcaded balcony that runs right around the patio.

Las Dueñas
SEVILLE

LAS DUEÑAS WAS BOUGHT BY THE RIBERA FAMILY, OWNERS OF THE CASA DE PILATOS, AT THE end of the fifteenth century for one of two brothers and, to avoid sibling rivalry, their mother, Catalina de Ribera, modified it so that to all intents and purposes the two grand houses would be identical. But to the modern eye, any similarity is historical and generic because the two households could not be more different.

Whereas the first patio of Casa de Pilatos is deliberately austere and grand with its marble paving, Renaissance fountain and classical busts, designed to impress and impose, the patio at Las Dueñas, which was originally also tiled with marble, is filled with colour and flower and, whilst impressive, seduces, invites and delights in equal measure.

As you look through the arch from the darkness of the *apeadero*, where visitors dismounted from their horses or coach, the patio glows with golden light reflected from the earthy yellow of the *albero*-coloured walls set off by highly patterned and ornate Moorish stone decoration. Whereas the patio at Casa de Pilatos is either intimidating or asking to be rollerbladed on, according to your status, this patio is filled with a myrtle-hedged parterre, the triangular beds planted with roses, their pointed ends facing in to the central fountain rising above a glazed and painted tiled base where yellow and blue glazed pots filled with pelargoniums line the rim. The pulsing magenta intensity of bougainvillea in its brief floral prime spills down from two rooftop corners of the patio. There are no Roman or classical sculptures or influences here with their refined stone austerity and Renaissance allusions. This is pure Andalusian, with its deep Moorish roots of colour, ornate decoration and craftsmanship filtered by nineteenth- and twentieth-century aristocratic grandeur.

Two enormous date palms rise to the height of the corner tower, their fronds spread in a glaucous fountain against the blue of the April sky and two smaller ones splay out against the *albero*. A large *Cassine orientalis* – East Indian olive – fills a corner.

This is the household of the Dukes of Alba but although its history is long and exceedingly grand, everything here is dominated by the presence of Cayetana Fitz-James Stuart, eighteenth Duchess of Alba. She was the most titled aristocrat in the world, also one of the richest, owned more land than the Spanish royal family and was, by any measure, a huge character famous for her parties, extravagance, marriages and eccentricities.

I first visited in winter 2013 whilst she was still alive and the house not open to the public. My wife and I were spirited around via a personal connection on a cold February day, the garden bleak and the house ghostly with her absence, her large collection of Mickey Mouse memorabilia daily dusted, the rooms closed but poised for her return. In fact she returned to die in the palace the following year at the age of 88, still eccentric, still adored by the people of Seville.

Above: The Patio del Aceite, where olive oil was originally kept in huge jars, has three towering date palms and a sago palm, considerably smaller than its companions but reckoned to be the oldest sago palm in the whole of Spain.

Opposite: The building glows a deep gold through the traditional – and very typically of Seville – *albero* wall colour.

Overleaf: The combination of the deep ochre, the ornate plasterwork, the green of the hedges and the vertical lines of columns and palm trees makes the entrance patio of Las Dueñas breathtakingly rich.

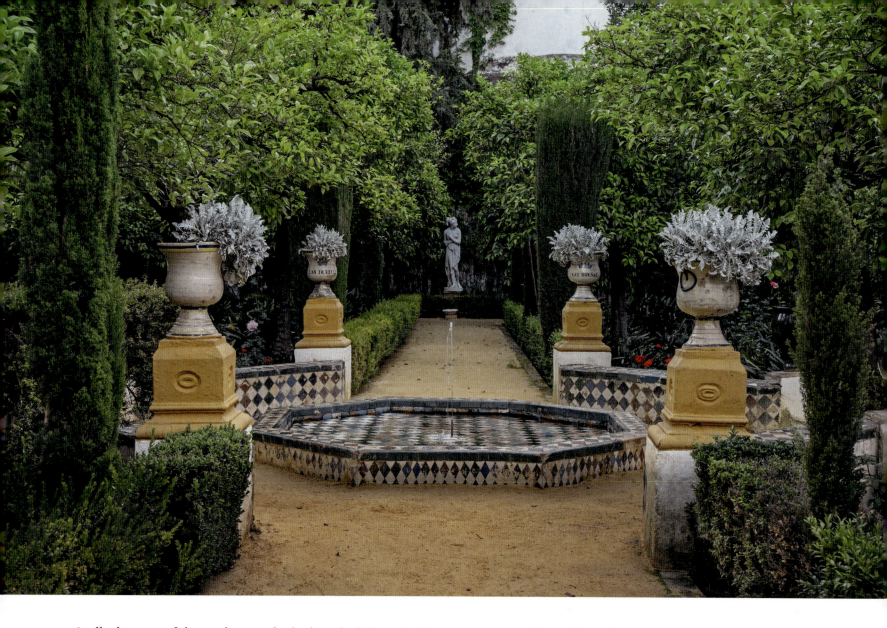

I talked to one of the gardeners who had worked there for the past 35 years and he told me that she loved the garden and particularly loved colour, and would plant favourite plants more or less at random. The palace once claimed to have 100 patios but these are now reduced to a mere seven, albeit amounting to a large, grand garden right in the heart of the city.

The Patio del Aceite, where olive oil was kept in huge jars, has three towering date palms and a sago palm, considerably smaller than its companions but reckoned, I was assured, to be the oldest sago palm in the whole of Spain. A large black glass and steel external lift imposed into one corner adds a jarring note but the heavy matting blinds are rolled halfway up the windows, ready to drop as a barrier against the Andalusian afternoon heat, looking as though they or their ilk have been there as long as the sixteenth-century glazed pool in the centre of the patio.

The Patio de los Limones is the largest and most central, which takes the Moorish and medieval idea of an orchard as an integral and precious part of a garden rather than the modern tendency

The Patio de los Limones is essentially an ornate orchard in the Islamic tradition, albeit with sculptures and vases that are distinctly Christian and post-Islamic.

The rich green leaves of pots of clivias and box hedging are the perfect foil to the gold of the building.

to see orchards as peripheral, semi-agricultural spaces. In fact it is bounded by the high white walls of neighbouring buildings, as urban a setting as could be contrived, and was created by buying neighbouring buildings and demolishing them to extend the garden. The lemon trees, underplanted with clivias, divided into four *charbagh* beds around a central shallow tiled pool and fountain, touch canopy to canopy, creating a green umbrella of fragrant shade.

Leading off to one side are the stables where six extra-large mules from Jerez were being groomed to a shining chestnut gleam, ready to pull the current duke's carriage in the following day's *feria*.

Here, with the narrow streets full of cars, people going to and from work and middle-aged tourists dressed like toddlers, is the extraordinary world of a ducal household, with its grooms, cooks, gardeners, housekeepers and no doubt many other retainers, like a large country estate distilled down to city size.

The whole garden is rich with colour, from brightly glazed tiles around fountains, blue and white pots with 'Las Dueñas' and the ducal coronet emblazoned on them, huge ornate plates and posters on walls as well as from the inevitable bougainvillea, jasmine, roses and the gleaming fruit of the orange trees. There are seats everywhere, not so much for the public but because the duchess liked to sit and entertain all around the garden, and, above all, that indefinable quality of personality that can only come from a powerful human connection.

The truth is that the duquesa is still everywhere in the building and in every corner of the garden. Prospero, the gardener I talked to, said that he looked after the garden for her so that if she was looking down, she would see that it was kept just as she liked it. In doing so, honouring her living memory, every visitor cannot help but like it too.

Opposite: Shade is the greatest luxury in the astonishing heat of Seville and the covered arcade around the patio, for all its grandeur, is a practical necessity.

Left: A customised pot filled with the glaucous foliage of senecio. Every aspect of the house and garden is integrated into a proud ducal fiefdom like a grand country estate but within and constrained by the narrow streets of the city.

Index

Acknowledgements

My thanks to all the owners of private gardens and custodians of public ones across Spain that gave us access and their time.

In particular, Piru Urquijo was an invaluable source of contacts, giving us access to a number of private gardens – not least her own at Los Molinillos. She was also a wonderfully generous host.

Cristina Martín and Carlos González Fernández were both a great help in researching gardens and organising logistics right across the country.

At Ebury, thanks to Albert De Petrillo who guided the book from conception to publication, Katie Fisher for editing my text with sensitivity and skill, and Andrew Barron for his layout design.

My agent and friend Alexandra Henderson guided, cajoled and encouraged me at every stage far beyond the call of any duty.

At home, my assistant Polly James did a huge amount to organise each journey but, as ever, my greatest gratitude is to my wife Sarah for holding our world together.

MONTY DON

As always in a book of this kind there are many people to whom I owe thanks. Should I have omitted to thank anyone I hope he or she will forgive me.

To all the owners of the various properties featured in the book, I am indebted for having allowed me to photograph their gardens. Without their help there would obviously have been no book at all.

I feel deeply indebted to Piru Urquijo, who extended such hospitality to us, not only allowed us to feature her garden but also introduced us to several other garden owners.

I would like to thank Katie Fisher and Albert De Petrillo at Ebury Publishing and Andrew Barron, who has shown great patience with our constant changes to the layout and achieved a wonderful result. Also Lucía Sebastià Salvadores, who drove me in Spain, and especially Cosmo Robinson, who not only drove me in Andalucía and the north but assisted me and made sure I took the necessary photographs – as well as being a delightful companion.

As always, it has been a huge pleasure working with Monty Don.

My assistants, Raffaella Matrone and Lucy Gooder, have been tremendously helpful and Brent Wallace has performed his usual magic when necessary.

Finally, special thanks to my wife, Alexandra, and daughter, Marina, whose help in selecting and editing the photographs has been invaluable.

DERRY MOORE

MONTY DON O.B.E. is the UK's leading garden writer and broadcaster. He has been lead presenter of *Gardeners' World* since 2003 and since 2011 the programme has come from his own garden, Longmeadow, in Herefordshire. He has written a weekly gardening column for the *Daily Mail* since 2004, and published over 20 books, including the bestsellers *Down to Earth*, *Nigel: My Family and Other Dogs* and *My Garden World*. *Japanese Gardens*, his book with Derry Moore, was shortlisted for the Edward Stanford Travel Writing Awards.

DERRY MOORE is an acclaimed photographer known for his images of gardens, houses, and architectural interiors and also for his portraits. His photographs have been reproduced in numerous magazines including *Architectural Digest*, *Vogue*, *Town and Country* and he has published several books including *Horses*, *The English Room*, and several books with Monty Don, including *Great Gardens of Italy*, *Paradise Gardens*, *Japanese Gardens*, *American Gardens* and *Venetian Gardens*.

I

BBC Books, an imprint of Ebury Publishing
Penguin Random House UK
One Embassy Gardens, 8 Viaduct Gardens,
Nine Elms, London SW11 7BW

BBC Books is part of the Penguin Random House group of companies
whose addresses can be found at global.penguinrandomhouse.com

Penguin
Random House
UK

The photo on p. 50 shows Jeff Koons' *Puppy*, 1992, stainless steel, soil,
geotextile fabric, internal irrigation system, and live flowering plants,
486 x 486 x 256 inches / 1234.4 x 1234.4 x 650.2 cm
© Jeff Koons

First published by BBC Books in 2024

www.penguin.co.uk

A CIP catalogue record for this book is available from the British Library

ISBN 9781785948725

Publishing Director: Albert De Petrillo
Editors: Nell Warner & Katie Fisher
Design: Andrew Barron
Photography: Derry Moore
Cartography: Cedric Knight

Printed and bound by Firmengruppe APPL,
aprinta druck, Wemding, Germany
Colour origination by Altaimage, London

The authorized representative in the EEA is Penguin Random House
Ireland, Morrison Chambers, 32 Nassau Street, Dublin D02 YH68

Penguin Random House is committed to a sustainable future for our
business, our readers and our planet. This book is made from Forest
Stewardship Council® certified paper.

FSC
www.fsc.org
MIX
Paper | Supporting
responsible forestry
FSC® C018179